# A Pivotal Time

## *Memoirs of Childhood in Small Town America After the War*

D1737261

# Martha Jennings

**For Barb and Jim**

# Contents

# *Foreword*

W hat is it about American small towns...places without skyscrapers or subways...the hamlets set against mountain ranges or nestled near lakes? There are thousands of them, you know...the settings just right for classic novels, mystery stories or coming-of-age memoirs. These are places where it's safe for kids to roam all day...where moms say: "Just be home when the street lights come on" with no need for worry. This is where people don't lock their doors and the police know everybody's dad, mom, brother, sister, aunts and uncles and even the family dog.

Celebrated developer, scholar, author, and champion of small communities, Arthur Morgan once wrote for the *Atlantic* in 1942 that small towns are the "seedbeds of society." He said the small community, whether rural or embedded within a metropolis, is where "the roots of civilization"..."elemental traits—goodwill, neighborliness, fair play, courage, tolerance, open minded inquiry, patience"…are best modeled and passed on from one generation to the next. But exactly *how* does this conveyance play out?…within what *context*?…by what *means*?

*A Pivotal Time* is a collection of stories from my personal experience...a tiny peek at some answers to these questions...specific events that expanded perspectives and shaped future directions for people in one particular southwestern Michigan small town. This is about a little village with a funny name and a cast of characters who lived, loved, labored, laughed and otherwise enjoyed a few decades together in mid-twentieth century America. All accounts are absolutely true and I think any speculation on my part found within them is pretty clearly identified as such. My fact checkers have agreed with a curt, "Yeah, Mart. That's just the way it happened. You have captured it for sure." So this is the way it was—the way Morgan's "roots of civilization" played out during one short span of time in my hometown, Paw Paw, Michigan. Enjoy!


Mart Jennings, 2020
Springfield, Massachusetts

# *'Legacies'*

Van Buren County is my home. The towns, the roads, the lakes, the vineyards, the orchards...they all speak to me and as I grow older, the message grows louder and clearer: "Van Buren County shaped you, your values, the rules that guide your life. Van Buren County is where you belong, your heritage."

The word *'heritage'* first entered my personal lexicon during the Paw Paw Village Centennial Celebration of 1959. Eisenhower was president then, the country was enjoying a surge of prosperity unthinkable just a generation before and for one week in late August the streets were alive both day and night. Carnival rides, barkers and cotton candy vendors spread out all over South Kalamazoo Street in front of the Carnegie Library building. Merchants sold their wares up and down main street on the sidewalks and a pageant played out every night at Tyler Field behind the high school. The story of Paw Paw's earliest settlers was reenacted there with oodles of townsfolk taking part. And, yes, even I had a small walk-on role at age eleven. The program titled "Footpaths to Freeways," was orchestrated by the John B. Rogers Producing Company. This outfit was based in Fostoria, Ohio, and made big business out of traveling the countryside supplying communities just like Paw Paw with costumes, performers, songs and instruction about how to pull off big centennial parties.

One of the most important items produced that summer under Rogers Company direction is a 65-page pictorial history souvenir. It's a book containing lists of pageant participants, ads for local businesses, photos of early Paw Paw scenes and an account of village growth written by local historian Harry Bush.

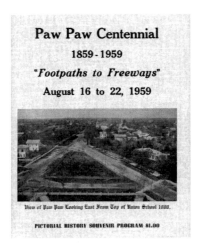

Paw Paw
Centennial
Program

Bush's narrative describes the big westward migration after the War of 1812. The British were forced out by colonial patriots. The borders were secured and pioneers flocked to Michigan territory in droves. Yankees from New England and New York came by way of the St. Lawrence River or the Erie Canal to buy up land once owned by native tribes. Easterners knew that Michigan soil was fertile. They also knew that a territorial road through the southern counties was planned and promised to open trade routes for farm goods. This meant there would be a good chance at prosperity for families living nearby. So they traveled old narrow footpaths along the proposed route and claimed land as they went. Trees were felled to make passages just wide enough for ox wagons to pass. Lots of stumps remained and made the going slow and bumpy. Yet they pressed ahead. Some ox wagons had four wheels, some had two. They were usually covered with canvas to protect passengers and cargo from the elements and moved at about 4 miles an hour while people walked alongside. Ann Arbor was settled and then incorporated in 1824. Kalamazoo followed in 1829 with Battle Creek in 1831. Further west, Paw Paw became a village in 1859.

One hundred years later, John B. Rogers found his markets for centennial pageantry by retracing territorial road routes east to west and advertising to communities formed along the way all over the heartland. What a neat idea! Rogers packaged plans for themes and events, then left space for each community to fill in the blanks with their own local lore. There were "best beard" competitions and Kangaroo Kourts to levy fines on those who shaved without a permit. The locals went about their business on the streets dressed in period costumes. The ladies wore sunbonnets, the gents sported bowlers and sack coats and Rogers arranged it all. At age eleven, I couldn't appreciate the full meaning of these events. Yet I do remember the costumes and the old-time apple butter we made in summer school just the way the settlers did. So in the wake of it, a tiny seed of awareness about local heritage was firmly planted with me way back then.

Sixty years after the centennial, more and more relatives fill the old burial grounds in Lawrence and Bangor. At each graveyard visit I notice recognizable names and dates etched in stone and just recently came to realize that my heritage seed is now grown to maturity. "Aha!" I said to myself. "These were the very people who arrived in Van Buren County by ox-drawn wagon during the original migration." These women wore the sunbonnets, made the apple butter and gave birth to my great grandparents on those early homesteads Harry Bush wrote about. These men drove the oxen, they wore the beards and cleared densely-forested Michigan land for planting. The migrants we celebrated in 1959 were *my* people...not some abstract group. They were real, they walked and talked and laughed and cried and they belonged to *me!* What an epiphany! Well...I guess sometimes it takes me quite a while to appreciate the obvious.

It's lucky for me that genealogy is all the rage right now. DNA testing and digitized data bases make short work of what used to be grueling searches through libraries and court houses sometimes at great distances from home. Now, technology makes the search a comparative cinch. People want to know where they came from and just like John B. Rogers, today's digital entrepreneurs have found a way to capitalize on that. I want to know my people too. Not just their birth and death dates, but where they came from, what their life was like and what motivated them. Could I possibly do that? I decided to try.

My DNA test came out as I expected except for a little French blood that somehow got mixed in with the English, Irish,

Scotch and German. Our family oral histories never mentioned anything about a French connection. I was intrigued and started searching. The first step was a family tree. It's pretty easy. I just started out with birth and death dates and all kinds of data came up online. Most of it was free and I worked from the couch. The only hard part was time and persistence. This is for sure not something I could do while holding down a full-time job. Many nights, fully engrossed and excited, I was up until the wee hours. The lineage was that interesting and I let it lead me all the way back to ancient England. But most of the time, I set a boundary and stopped at 1620 when I found the Mayflower connections. Yup! I'm one of 35 million descendants, 10% of the U.S. population and Plymouth Rock came up on both sides. Mom and Dad would be blown away to know this and so am I. I never thought about it before, but with more and more research it makes perfect sense. The people who settled Michigan came from the east! New England! And who settled New England? Connect the dots!! It was yet another Aha! moment for me. Read on for a clearer picture.

After arrival at Plymouth and other ports nearby, Mom's people broke off to settle in the Connecticut and Thames River valleys. By 1775, they had traveled up the Connecticut and into Western Massachusetts in search of more and more land. This was the time of the First Continental Congress in Philadelphia and the signing of the Declaration of Independence in 1776. During the Revolution, these folks fought for our independence then made their way west across New York, settling in the Buffalo area by 1820. The Wattles family made the journey then through Detroit and westward to finally settle in Portage, Michigan between 1834 and 1840. Mom descended from these folks in Kalamazoo four generations later.

The Wattles may have been on the road at the very same time that Dad's people traveled from New York around 1836. These folks had solid roots in Massachusetts before pushing west and once they reached Michigan, they went a bit past Kalamazoo to eventually find homesteads in Clinch, the original name for Almena Township. Benjamin Eager made the journey to Van Buren County following the death of his wife Sally Ball Brigham Eager. Benjamin and Sally married in 1805 in Boylston,

Massachusetts. He was 26 and she 14. For certain, Sally was pregnant and this was a big scandal in Boylston. I suppose it was made especially so because Benjamin was the son of a clergyman, Sally the daughter of a physician and of all the stories uncovered during my searches, this one about these two lovers touches me most deeply. They were kids when George Washington was president. They got married when Thomas Jefferson anguished, after the fact, about his Louisiana Purchase and sent Lewis and Clark on their voyage of discovery to check it out. Then Ben and Sally expired while Abraham Lincoln was working his way to the White House. They lived through all that.

After about 10 or 12 years of marriage in Massachusetts, Benjamin and Sally Eager headed out some two hundred miles north with their seven children to St. Albans and Swanton, Vermont, far away from their original home and families. Then sometime between 1830 and 1832 they made another bold move, this time westward to the wilderness of Franklin County New York. It appears this Benjamin Eager was a very venturesome man. Perhaps it was an opportunity in logging too attractive to pass up. Or maybe they were both adventurers. Whatever the case, it was in Franklin County that Sally gave birth to her last child in February 1832 and then expired the following May at age 42. The reason for death is unclear. It could have been illness. Cholera was a problem at that time. Maybe it was an injury. Or maybe she just couldn't keep up. Certainly the stress of bearing and caring for 14 children starting at the age of 14 herself must have taken a toll. The epitaph on Sally's grave marker reads:

Eager
Sacred to the memory of Sally B. Consort of Benj. Eager
Died May 31, 1832 in the 42 year of her age.
Her mind was tranquil and serene
No terror in her looks were seen
Her saviour's smile dispelled the gloom
and smoothed her passage to the tomb.

Without reading too much into this, the passage implies Sally was anticipating death. It also suggests that whoever chose the passage did so with   care.   I am moved by the tone and I wonder about the Lutheran origins of this verse.   Were they Lutherans?   There is no way to know.   But I am relieved that she is not buried there alone.   A separate stone in the same lot is for Sally's third child to die too soon:

Harriet A. Daughter of Benj. & Sally B. Eager
Died April 2, 1844 in the 21 year of her age.

It is interesting that Ben's siblings chose not to move around as Ben and Sally did.   They stayed at home in Massachusetts.   The same is true of Sally's people.   Ben and Sally, it seems, could have been "black sheep."   Ben  never remarried and this was *not* the usual thing.   Most men who lost their wives in those days looked around for replacements right away. Instead, it appears Ben preferred to put his energy and family resources into pioneering.   He waited  four years following Sally's death until daughter Sarah was 17, probably in his mind old enough to look after her younger siblings and sister Martha, two years younger, would soon be able to help.   Then he set out for the northwest frontier. When he got to Michigan,  he immediately started buying up land and lots of it.

I am inclined to think this was a well-laid plan. He traveled with a few of his older children who could help him get a solid start and build their own homesteads.   At first glance, it seems harsh of Ben to leave the young ones behind, but it appears that there was support to be had from older siblings still living nearby while Ben went on westward into the wilderness to prepare a place for those who wanted to follow. By staying behind, the younger ones had a chance to mature, become educated within the relative civilization of the east and find suitable mates at home before following westward still having enough time left by then to make a go of life with their family in Michigan. It looks like this was Ben's reasoning, considering the way they followed him.   Seven of his nine living children, it seems, thought enough of him to trust his judgment or just wanted to be close to him and then convinced their spouses to make the trek. My great-great-grandmother, Ben's daughter Martha, traveled with her husband Herman Sanborn and arrived before 1853 with the first five of their own twelve children. They settled in Paw Paw just soon enough to spend time with Ben before he died in 1854 at age 79.

Ben is buried at Almena Cemetery below a headstone that bears the word "Grandpa" across the top in bold raised letters. It may be that this type of marker was the custom at the time, but I prefer to think this is proof of the tender sentiments Ben's grandchildren felt toward him and testament to the kind of man he must have been to earn those feelings.

Martha Ann Eager Sanborn must have been tough as nails.
She is about 50 years old here. Photo probably taken about 1870. She lost an eye somewhere along the way and if she were smiling, there were most likely a few teeth missing too. She and Herman are buried at Prospect Lake Cemetery in Lawrence not far from other relatives.

The way I view it, this is quite a love story. Two nonconformists, making the most of opportunities, taking a chance on their passions and each other ....WOW!! It didn't work out well for Sally, but it looks as though Ben was a devoted husband, determined to see their dream through and provide the best he could muster for his progeny. He certainly left a wonderful story to ponder and I am glad I discovered the remnants of it. By little bits and pieces and on some new level, these folks have come alive again and I now know my people.

How many other stories of migrant heritage are yet to be told by folks just like me.....folks who ramble around old family burial grounds, dig through historical texts, uncover lost stories and want to leave a legacy for those who come after? I bet it's a bunch…stories left to be told by we folks who know that Van Buren County is where we belong.

# 'Where have you gone, Ed Murrow?'

As I write, the TV set is on low volume in the next room, tuned to one of maybe two hundred cable channels. Who on earth needs two hundred TV channels? We might use five or six of them—just a few more than we had in Paw Paw during the early days of television some seventy years ago. My sister Kay was around eight or nine in 1949 and is certain that we had a set by then. Those were the days when TV broadcast licensing was growing across the nation at almost breakneck speed, with only 20% of American households owning a set in 1950 and increasing to 90% by 1960. The price of a set early on was about $250! That's the equivalent of well over $2,000 today and an awful lot of money...at least for our family. I don't know how our folks managed to buy it. Mom stayed home with Kay and me until I was four or five. She and Dad usually managed to provide what we needed, but in our household, in that era, a price tag that size for anything was a huge extravagance. Still, they somehow scraped enough cash together, maybe by skimping on other things or by paying in installments. Whatever the case, Kay said it seemed they "just had to have it." All their friends had one. They couldn't miss out!

We had several sets during the years I lived at home and all were purchased from G.R. Marcelletti, owner of the Record Shop on Main Street. Marcelletti's showroom was packed with mostly console models. They looked like pieces of furniture and we could get one that fit our decor. There were rows and rows to choose from and Marcelletti serviced them too. Yes, TV service was a huge part of owning a set. They were built using vacuum tubes of various sizes with short durabilities and made Marcelletti a very busy and popular man in town. When a tube blew out and the picture went dark, we were in for a wait of several days before G.R.'s van appeared in our driveway. Service required diagnosis and replacement of the burned out tube. I don't know how much he charged for a service call, but I do know that my folks hoped and prayed that the big picture tube was not part of the problem. Picture tube replacements were the most expensive of breakdown problems.

Marcelletti was a friendly man as I recall and came into the house toting a black case loaded with new tubes. The case was huge-maybe even as big as I was and it unfolded like a tackle box. He pulled the set away from the wall, looked inside from the back and located the culprit tube. Then he selected from his case a brand new replacement and we were back in business. He always left the burned-out tubes behind and I remember inspecting them carefully. They looked kind of like light bulbs but with straight sides instead of curved and pins at the bottom that fit into chassis holes that matched the pins on the tube. I was fascinated!

Yes indeed, it seemed all of us were fascinated with everything about television. Once the set was running again, it was as if our household breathed a collective sigh of relief. Being without TV, even in those early years, was an unwelcome or even dreaded privation. We came to depend on it that quickly. TV was a game changer—a window on the world around us, near and far. When television was present, isolation was banished and all of America shared a common experience. Our broadcast ranges let us receive signals from a CBS affiliate in Kalamazoo, and a station in Grand Rapids affiliated with NBC. Yes, we had only those two channels. Programming schedules started around six a.m. and went off the air at about midnight. Kids' shows followed the news in the early morning, soap operas, usually sponsored by detergent manufacturers, ran in the afternoon, and network news came on around dinner time. At some point, maybe about 1958 to 1962, old movies from the '30's and '40's were featured in the mid-afternoon and I binged on them during school vacations. I loved that stuff!

They taught me a lot about the pre-war era, Mom and Dad's younger years.

After dinner in the evenings during the years before I had homework from school, TV was a family activity, something we shared. We only had one set, so we were together. Sometimes I climbed up into Mom's big upholstered arm chair to cuddle or sat on the couch with Dad. Usually though, I preferred a place on the floor where I could play with toys as we watched and talked about what we were seeing on the small screen. There was something special for everyone. Dad loved sports coverage. His sport in school was football and he followed all the games, the plays, the moves. He liked Friday night fights too. He could be there without the bother of travel, expensive tickets or the headaches of fighting the crowd. Both Mom and Dad liked the dramas on *Playhouse 90*, the variety shows like *Ed Sullivan* and of course *I Love Lucy*.

*Playhouse 90* catered to the high brow crowd with ninety minute stage plays written and performed, sometimes live, for the elites with a taste for excellence in theatre. These shows came on later in the evening, after my bedtime. But the staircase in our house was directly opposite the living room TV set and out of Mom and Dad's line of vision, so I sometimes sneaked down to sit on the steps just to see what all the fuss was about. I usually grew weary after only five or ten minutes and put myself back to bed. *Playhouse 90*, I found, was not my cup of tea at age five.

*The Ed Sullivan Show,* on the other hand, was the creation of a sports and entertainment news columnist of the same name. Sullivan's program was originally titled *Toast of the Town* and started out early on TV (around 1948). It was a Sunday night hour-long collection of comedy, dance, music and drama featuring established and new performers from all genres. The show ran for twenty-three years and could make or break a performing career. So artists coveted spots on Sullivan's stage and did their best to comply with his wishes. The show aired from 8-9 p.m., a family viewing time, and parents trusted that Ed Sullivan would book wholesome entertainment, appropriate for kids to see. Still, Sullivan was under pressure to keep up with popular demand and finally agreed to feature the new and somewhat controversial rock-and-roll sensation Elvis Presley. Qualms about the booking centered on Presley's enthusiasm for singing "jumpy" tunes while moving his lower extremities in ways that some viewers thought too suggestive or even "vulgar."

But the crowds loved Elvis, so Sullivan hosted Presley's group three times and dealt with the issue during their last appearance by zooming the camera in so tight that Elvis' image was only visible from his waist up. Even at age 8, I too was caught up in the rage over Elvis and Mom let me watch. I witnessed his gyrations during one of the first two shows and frankly I don't think I suffered any ill effects from it---just happiness at sharing in the experience of seeing and hearing the teen idol do his thing.

Then there was *I Love Lucy*. It was a situation comedy starring red headed former model and movie star turned comedienne, Lucille Ball and her Cuban born bandleader husband, Desi Arnaz. The duo was a curiosity for the era. Networks were wary about casting such a couple. Executives doubted that American audiences could warm to what might be perceived as a biracial union. But all qualms in this case too were quickly abandoned. *I Love Lucy* became the most watched television show for four of its six seasons between 1951 until 1957. In fact, the original shows can still be seen in syndication today, over 60 years later.

Ball was a trailblazer, one of just a few women of the era to take on a comedy persona and she did it brilliantly. With a style that might be described as slap stick, the show featured mischievous antics with Lucy and her landlady pal, Ethel Mertz, to the amazement and exasperation of their husbands, Ricky and Fred. I think I enjoyed watching. Again, we did this as a family. Mom and Dad liked *Lucy* and I liked being with them. But some of the sketches were a stretch for me. I was only five or six when I saw one episode in which Lucy got herself locked in an industrial-sized freezer. Rather than seeing this scene with it's intended humor, I was afraid for Lucy's safety. I guess my sense of empathy was pretty keen as a little one. This episode of so-called "family friendly viewing" on *Lucy* ultimately proved much more traumatic for me than Elvis' suggestive gyrations. Well, so much for censorship guidelines in those days.

My memories of watching all these things with Mom and Dad are a treasure, but the biggest attraction for me of course was the kid's programming. The first one I recall clearly was *Howdy Doody*. It must have been about 1953. The buckskin-clad Master of Ceremonies, Buffalo Bob, called out, "Hey kids, what time is it?" to the Peanut Gallery on stage. The bunch of kids in the gallery called back, "It's Howdy Doody time!" Then marionettes Howdy Doody and his pals Princess Summer Fall Winter Spring and an ornery old dude named Mr. Bluster appeared and carried on with Bob, the kids, and Clarabelle, the clown.

In the fall of 1955, Walt Disney decided to take his popular cartoon character and kid's club concept to the airwaves with a cadre of clean cut "Mouseketeers" as hosts. The original *Mickey Mouse Club* ran for four years, Monday through Friday at five o'clock. For at least the first year or two, my neighborhood best friend Johnny Fleming and I never missed it. Usually seated cross-legged style on Rita Fleming's hand braided living room rag rug, we munched on carrot and celery sticks, sang along, and savored every story.

All the above and much more came to be known as the "Golden Age of Television." The performers came from already-established careers maybe from Broadway, Vaudeville or journalism. TV offered a new venue for them and expanded their visibility many times over. For the first time, live world-class visual entertainment was accessible within the comfort of home, and this was big! It was big for the artists, big for the viewers, but also big for program sponsors and it didn't take long for corporate America to cash in.

Saturday morning viewing had a huge target market for breakfast cereals that appealed to children. There was nonstop kid's programming from 8 a.m. until noon. Cornflakes, oatmeal, cream of wheat and bran cereals from Kellogg's, C.W. Post and others were staples for decades before that. But in 1952, Tony the Tiger appeared as mascot when Kellogg's came out with a sugary product called Frosted Flakes and the race was on. Sometimes packages came with a toy or book inside. Then if Mom bought enough Frosted Flakes, Sugar Pops, Rice Krispies or other sweet breakfast food, we could send in box tops with maybe twenty-five cents and receive a neat toy through the mail. Kay and I got a set of Snap, Crackle and Pop hand puppets that way and a plastic submarine that submerged and resurfaced all by itself with a little help from a half teaspoonful of baking powder in its hull. That was pretty exciting stuff for a four- or five-year-old! And what a sales scheme! Kids were bugging their moms to buy in bulk. Imagine how many packages went flying off the shelves just to collect enough box tops to get a little piece of plastic in return.

Tobacco companies found their markets with evening shows like *I Love Lucy*. Phillip Morris' mascot was a uniformed, pillbox-capped bellboy. The slogan: "Call-for-Phil-ip-Mor-aze" was broadcast by the clear-voiced lad (actually a small middle-aged man) at the opening of the show. The symbolism was wasted on viewers my age. I had no frame of reference for understanding how this phrase nor the bellboy image could possibly be related to cigarettes. But Mom and Dad were both smokers and, of course, more worldly than I. They knew about bellboys and paging techniques in hotel lobbies, so I guess they could relate. Actually, I was an *unwitting* smoker at age five since most people didn't know anything about secondary smoke in those days. I'm sure Mom and Dad would be horrified to know that they were poisoning my immediate airspace, the very place they were otherwise trying to keep safe from harm.

Smoking was common and actually romanticized in those days. The old movies from the '30s and '40s included a lot of puffing and I understand that Lucky Strikes were packaged with C rations for our troops during WWII. Cigarette smoking on the big screen carried over to TV shows too. Celebrated war-correspondent-turned-commentator Edward R. Murrow was rarely if ever seen without a lit cigarette while broadcasting his groundbreaking weekly program, *See It Now*. The lit cigarette became Murrow's trademark and ultimately the cause of his early death at age 57 from lung cancer. Word is, he routinely smoked three packs a day.

Mom quit her habit cold-turkey when our doctor, Charlie TenHouten, told her to. TenHouten told Dad to quit too but he was addicted and just couldn't do it. Dad died at age 54 of colon cancer. Even after that diagnosis, he was still puffing away until his last breath in 1969.

Yeah, sponsors were hawking sugary diets for kids and carcinogenic inhalants for their parents, yet TV advertising practices proved to have an even darker side than that and it came to public attention through the quiz show scandals of the 1950s. Most notable among these was the revelation that cosmetic sponsor Revlon, Inc. methodically rigged *The $64,000 Question* game show by coaching favored contestants in advance of each game. The ploy was intended as a way to boost viewer numbers, ratings, and thereby product sales. No laws against cheating in this way existed at the time, so no one went to jail, but public trust was gravely compromised. TV fans felt deceived, reputations were stained, the big jackpot quiz shows were discontinued and, in 1960, Congress amended the Communications Act of 1934 to assure that sort of thing never happened again. It was a big deal. We were vulnerable and needed protection. But who would provide it?

Maybe coincidentally or maybe not, around the time the quiz show scandals were in full public view, our war-correspondent-turned-commentator Ed Murrow, delivered one of the most enduring messages of his career. It was 1958 at the Radio and Television News Directors Association Convention in Chicago. I was in the fifth grade then, maybe ten years old and have no memory of that famous speech, yet it has been referenced enough in my reading and repeated so often in movies and newsreels that I almost feel as if I was right there as he spoke. The content tells us he was worried. He was worried that the miracles of TV and radio were being squandered and even misused for ..."decadence, escapism and insulation from the realities of the world in which we live." Murrow cautioned his news journalism colleagues about the power of the new medium and implored them to apply it wisely. He then went on to challenge his peers. He wanted them to put more trust in the consumer. He said the public really wants and needs truthful, impactful reports on matters that affect their welfare, no matter how ugly that truth may be. He ended with a phrase quoted many times over since that day in 1958 and I suppose will be restated many times again over the generations to come. He said, "This instrument can teach, it can

15

illuminate; yes, and it can even inspire. But it can do so only to the extent that humans are determined to use it for those ends, otherwise it's nothing but wires and lights in a box...."

Murrow knew first hand how compelling TV could be as a social influence. He personally employed the power of *See It Now* in 1954 as a platform to rebuke Senator Joseph McCarthy. McCarthy, of course, was infamously censured by the Senate for abuse of power and that censure was, in large part, due to Murrow's factual rebuttal of claims made by the Senator. McCarthy falsely accused hundreds of government employees and other U.S. citizens of sympathizing with Russian communists and claimed they were conspiring to overthrow our government. Even our famous comedienne, Lucille Ball, and prominent physicist, Albert Einstein were on McCarthy's list of suspected subversives. Purging hearings went on from 1950 until 1954. There were indeed some actual Russian spies to be routed out, deported or otherwise removed. But untold numbers of innocent citizens were also accused and persecuted and careers and lives ruined by McCarthy's cruel tactics. Finally, when the TV cameras were trained on actual committee proceedings, McCarthy's abusive style was revealed to a shocked, disgusted and horrified nation and the nightmare came to a close.

Could Ed Murrow's rebuke of McCarthy and famous speech in Chicago make him our champion protector? Well, Murrow had a passion and a gift for seeking out and sharing, in no-nonsense style, the bare, unapologetic and sometimes unsavory facts of the day. He believed his style was what we deserved and that we could handle it and come to our own conclusions if armed with indisputable truth. We are lucky that we had him. He was an intellectual with lofty standards for his work and high expectations for most everyone else. Since Murrow's time, many fine men and women journalists have been inspired by his words and continue to meet his challenge for producing his brand of unvarnished, truthful reporting.

Murrow was one of the things that made the golden age of television a wondrous time. He was right. TV *can* seem decadent and escapist and, if we let it, can insulate us from the rest of the world. Yet in spite of these less-than-lofty intentions, I did learn from it as a youngster and continue to learn today. It presents new ideas and I am still inspired by many things I see and hear on TV. Except for those few moments with Lucy in the freezer, my memories of the golden age are happy...with family, friends, learning and fascination.

In some ways it was a simpler time. The technology was certainly simpler. Today, TV sets are made up of gases, metals, microchips and circuit boards instead of vacuum tubes and wires. And attitudes may have been simpler then too. I don't think Mom and Dad pondered too much about how the new medium might undermine their way of thinking. With advances in science and communication techniques, we have also acquired a higher level of sophistication about how we are influenced than was the norm 60 years ago. As I said earlier, how do we keep up with over 200 channels, including 24-hour news commentary from all sides of the political spectrum regularly bombarding our airwaves every day with all sorts of conflicting messages? Besides that, we have newer, maybe even more influential, communication devices doing the same thing in faster, more random fashion and Ed Murrow is not here to advocate for honesty on those platforms. Mom and Dad are gone too, so where shall we turn now for the big accurate picture? In whom shall we trust?

In thinking this through, my mind returns time and time again to some sage advice from my grandfather McKinstry upon the occasion of my Paw Paw High School graduation. On May 4, 1966 he wrote:

> *My Dear Sweetheart ....I hope that during the next momentous four years that you will learn to think and reason clearly and logically, and to be able to analyze what is worthwhile and what isn't, in this complicated life of ours... my dear, always be true to yourself and do what you and your conscience thinks best. Don't follow the herd just because everyone else does and thinks its the thing to do, do what you think is right and just...With so much love from Your Old Bapa*

My grandfather's counsel mirrors Murrow's message to his journalist peers. Mark McKinstry believed that consumers had what it takes to separate fact from fiction and then use what we find to make our own best decisions. Yet McKinstry went a little further than that. Whereas Murrow cited his colleagues' responsibility for truth in broadcasting, Grandfather McKinstry explicitly cited *my* responsibility ...*my* duty to myself and my community as a *recipient* of all messages. He challenged me to not blindly accept the claims or opinions of others. Instead, he insisted that I must care enough and use what I have learned to tease out the truth; to "think and reason......to analyze what is worthwhile and what isn't" for myself. Grandfather McKinstry's advice made me feel strong, confident and comforted in 1966 and more so today "in this [extremely] complicated life of ours." It's a different kind of comfort than I felt sitting on Rita Fleming's braided rag rug munching carrot and celery sticks with Johnny. But for today, it's just what I need.

# 'Dancing Heroes'

I am thinking lately about Liberty—the sea green lady who keeps silent watch over New York Harbor—the symbol of our sacred national concept—the cornerstone of our country's existence. She is not a given, you know. Liberty is vulnerable, under threat everyday and needs constant vigilant protection. We *obtained* her a long time ago through brave colonial struggle and gruesome bloody sacrifice. Then, just over one hundred years later, the "Greatest Generation" fought even more bloody battles to save her for you and me. I knew those folks—those who risked their lives for us. They were pals with Mom and Dad. Actually, they *were* Mom and Dad.

Barbara McKinstry and James Jennings met at a house party on Hazen Street overlooking Maple Lake. I think it was around 1939 or '40. He enlisted in '40, so maybe he was in uniform by then. Of course he was a charmer and probably swept her right off her feet. He was a star athlete in high school football and track at Paw Paw yet floundering about what he wanted to do with his life. I can't help but think he zeroed in on Mom's drive for excellence and her practical side. A Kalamazoo College grad in '38, looking to put her foreign language skills to work in the classroom, Barb McKinstry was classy, fun, smart, educated, competent, caring and responsible. What a catch! He asked her to marry him and Kay arrived in July of '41, six months before FDR declared war. The war postponed their honeymoon years as it did the plans of about sixteen million other young Americans in the prime of their lives. They all switched gears, came together and tended to the business of saving the world from tyranny until the job was done.

Master Sergeant James Jennings was with the Army Air Corps 343$^{rd}$ Bombardment Squadron--- a Line Chief in North Africa charged with making sure the planes were battle ready to carry flyers to their targets and get them back safely. He was decorated with the Legion of Merit for his role there servicing flights to Romania that destroyed Hitler's oil refineries at Ploesti.

That was exciting and harrowing work. But he never shared details and I had no sense of the drama until my research for this piece. Was it modesty? Did he just want to forget the horrors of war? I'll never know. He wouldn't talk about it. But as I understand from other WWII vets, they talked about the war only with comrades in arms. In some cases, the experience was so horrific and the aftermath so ridden with survivor's guilt, residual suffering may be the reason why so many of them turned to drink as their only way to keep the pain at bay. Mom of course, was on the homefront with a new baby, waiting and worrying for four long years.

The worldwide conflict occurred before I came along, but the cedar chest in our hallway upstairs at home held a treasure trove of clues about what their life was like during that terrifying time. I went through the uniforms, the air mail letters, the photo albums and other trinkets time and time again when I was small and then later as I grew and tried to understand their significance. Way down at the bottom of that chest were photos of Mom and Dad's veteran friends together at home with their spouses after the carnage. The images are frozen in time and in my mind: smiling, war weary young faces, glad they made it through, safely at home and savoring liberty once again. Some of my absolute favorites among those snapshots show a group of four couples: Mom and

Dad, Chuck and Joyce Sage, Ed and Peg Brennan and Mary Jeannett and Keith Stewart.

Left: Jim and Barb, Chuck and Joyce

Below: Ed and Peg, Mary Jeannette and Keith

Mary Jeannette's maiden name was Gilkey. Her Dad was a dentist in town and she went to school with Peg, Ed and Dad. Keith was from Ohio. I don't know much more about them, except that they came to visit occasionally. But I came to know the others quite well as they settled in to resume their lives and raise families in Paw Paw.

First Lieutenant Charles Sage was a fighter pilot with the Air Corps stationed in England. He flew 32 sorties over London and earned the Distinguished Flying Cross for his service defending the Brits from German aggression. Just imagine how scary that must have been! Chuck and Joyce met at Maple Island one summer day. She was on vacation from Jackson, Ohio, visiting her Aunt in Paw Paw. She noticed him sunbathing on the shore, struck up a chat and that was that! They married in 1944 after his discharge and were together for forty-two years until Chuck died from emphysema in 1986. I remember Joyce and Chuck best because of the Hotel de Hamburger, otherwise known around town as "Sage's," and the warm welcome I always got as a kid whenever I showed up there for one of their luscious burgers. Daughter Sherry, who happened to be in my class at school, tells me a good part of the secret behind those burgers had to do with the old grill used to cook them. I personally tend to think the bun steamer added a lot to the flavor, too. Chuck popped a bun in, gave the lever a couple of pumps and out came a perfectly soft, warm luscious roll for my burger. The patty recipe of course is the clincher, closely held and never revealed. Alas, Sherry says that she and her brothers have agreed they will carry it with them to the grave. So for all who ever tasted one of those wondrous sandwiches, know now that you are forever truly privileged and belong to a slowly dwindling minority. The "Sage Burger" is no more.

Ed Brennan was in Dad's class at Paw Paw. They played football together and were great pals. He went off to Notre Dame and the University of Chicago after high school and then returned to make a life for himself in his hometown when he was finished. Ed fancied the Air Corps too and it may be that he and Dad enlisted on the same day.

In all likelihood, Ed and Peg knew each other as kids. She was the only child of Dr. and Mrs. A.E. Van Vleck in Paw Paw and lived in the big white house with wrap-around front porch at the northeast corner of Brown and Main Streets. Peg was a year ahead of Ed and Dad in school and spent a year at Western Michigan University before she went south the next year to Stephens College in Columbia, Missouri. She finished up in Ann Arbor at U. of M.'s

College of Literature, Science and the Arts in 1936. From old records, it looks like she worked in Paw Paw for a while before they married in 1941.

Ed Brennan was a "take-charge" sort of fellow, someone who was always up for a gathering of good friends and this may be one of the reasons for his successful career in sales. Mom said it was Ed who arranged most of their parties and he was always on top of the latest and greatest of trends. Just before Bob Wade started offering rotisserie chickens at his Party Shop on West Main, Ed was one step ahead, roasting his own at home on his new patio barbecue spit for a gathering of the gang. I was there for one of those parties, probably around '56, and was actually transfixed for a few moments by the sight of that bird turning slowly round and round on a skewer above red hot coals. It was just about eye level for me at age seven or eight and a sight altogether new. I took in as much as my attention span could handle and then ran off to play with the other kids.

Ed's self-assured style showed up clearly, as I recall, when we were gathered at Thompson's Funeral Home during visitation hours for Dad in '69. He entered confidently, with certain purpose, crossed the room, sat immediately next to Mom on the couch, took her hand firmly in his and did not let go as they sat together talking quietly. Dad and Ed were buddies, comrades. I was struck by what I was seeing and will never forget it. Ed was grieving the loss of his lifelong pal and showed his sorrow and caring by taking his rightful place beside Dad's widow just as loyal brothers do. It was impressive.

Peg and Mom were close friends too. They shared cherished things, like membership at the First Presbyterian Church, excellence at the bridge table, having babies the same age, and living next door to each other on Birch lane.

Of course all these people were quite individual in character, but there was one special passion Mom, Dad and their veteran friends shared in common: they loved to dance. Their brand of music was the Big Band sound ...Glenn Miller, Harry James, Jimmy Dorsey, Ozzie Nelson, Count Basie. They did the foxtrot, waltz and the Lindy Hop, named for Charles Lindbergh after his famous transatlantic flight. These were the sounds they grew up with in the '30s, the Depression years. There was no TV and very little money, so dancing was the big attraction. Kids came together and, for a little while, did the fancy footwork and forgot about their troubles. It sure makes sense that after the fighting was over and the Allies prevailed, those same kids wanted to take up right where they left off, to recapture their happy times together with swing dance steps and Big Band sounds.

I have written elsewhere about the "Floating Front Porch," a scheme cooked up and executed by Dad and a few of his pals. And since then, the original newspaper account has resurfaced. I think it's worth including it here as an example of the fun they had and the extraordinary things they did during those early postwar years—these inventive folks known as the "Greatest Generation." The following piece is copyrighted, was originally published in the *Kalamazoo Gazette* sometime during the summer of 1949, and is reprinted with permission of *MLive Media Group/Kalamazoo Gazette:*

RAFT OF FUN
Paw Paw Ex-Gi's Build Their Own Stork Club
By DAN RYAN
*Does your income keep you fresh out of yachts?*
*Is your pocketbook too flat for nightclubing?*
*Nautically speaking, you aren't the only one in that boat. But if you follow the lead of a group of ex-Gi's in Paw Paw, you can make the boat into a raft of fun. Tired of tossing their money away in smoke-filled dining and dancing spots, the boys pooled their resources and know-how and are now the proud owners and crew of the U.S.S. Salvage, Michigan's only private floating club.*
*The Salvage was born during a discussion between Bill Warner, Chuck Sage and Jim Jennings, all army vets, over what to do with a war surplus rubber float purchased by Warner. "When I bought it," Warner says, "I thought it was going to be just a medium sized thing. But when we got it blown up it looked big enough to build a house on."*

*The original plan called for the laying of a plank floor over the boat to make a diving platform. But, like Topsy, "it just grew."*

*Jennings, who operates a sawmill, volunteered enough scrap lumber to make the floor. Sage and Warner scrambled around town and salvaged chunks of carpeting, canvas, pipe, rope and other odds and ends.*

Boasts Snack Bar, Dance Floor

*It's the Stork Club with no cover charge and a built-in breeze. As she floats now, the U.S.S. Salvage looks like a cross between an ocean-going yacht and a coal barge.*

*A 12 by 20 foot hardwood floor is laid across the big rubber boat. The floor is completely enclosed by a waist-high white pipe railing. The rear half of the floored area is canopied with bright green canvas which once adorned the front wall of a Paw Paw shoe store. Beneath the canopy is a handsome red leather snack bar.*

*The leather, which smacks of luxury, is actually scrap material from the Checker Cab Manufacturing corporation.*

*Built into the bar is an automobile radio powered by an automobile battery.*

*Deck chairs and smoking stands are scattered about the rear area which is carpeted with a slightly moth-eaten relic from someone's attic.*

*Trimmings include inflated inner tubes painted white for life preservers, flag poles fore and aft, running lights made from old kerosene lanterns, a mast and compass.*

*The group's only naval veteran, Bob Harrison, Paw Paw automobile salesman, is responsible for the more technical aspects of life about the "floating front porch".*

*"I hang the red light on the port side and green light on the starboard," he says. "After that it's every man for himself."*

Serves Two-fold Purpose

*The Salvage is serving a two-fold purpose so far. During the day the wives of the builders use it as a cool and comfortable site for sunbathing, bridge playing and sewing.*

*Every sunny afternoon babies are popped into carriages and wheeled aboard so the mothers can enjoy a visit together without needing babysitters.*

*Although the raft is unsinkable and will hold up a total of 12,000 pounds, the girls don't venture out in the lake with the children aboard. But even anchored in shallow water it beats any land-locked sun porch for fun and comfort.*

*In the evening the raft serves as a clubhouse for young couples seeking relief from the summer heat. Provisions are taken aboard, lines are cast off and an outboard motor pushes the strange looking craft out into the cool breezes of Maple Lake.*

*Once out from shore, the boys drop anchor, turn on the radio and dance, play bridge, fish or just relax. It's the Stork Club with no cover charge and a built in breeze.*

There is no question in my mind about how we won the war. Those guys just kept right on using their skills the way they did overseas and turned out super stuff. They had a great time on that make-shift pontoon boat. But it seems their time with the big play thing was short lived. Dan Ryan was wrong. The U.S.S. Salvage was *not* unsinkable. It's unclear what happened, but I suppose the rubber float sprang a leak. Safety codes in those days must have been lax or even non-existent. Thank God no one was hurt and we babies were not allowed out on the lake. Whew!! As I understand from Joyce Sage, the wreckage remains on the floor of Maple Lake to this day and the worst consequence was that the fun-loving dancing crowd was forced to find other venues.

Above, artist J. Belliveau's impressionistic rendering of the *Gazette* photo image which accompanied Dan Ryan's *Raft of Fun*. In the distance, vintage cars parked alongside M-40 belonged to Maple Isle patrons.

Babies who escaped the fate of the U.S.S. Salvage. That's me on the left with Mom, Barb. Then Sherry with Mom Joyce. Next is Bob Brennan with Grandma Warner and Barney Warner with Mom June.

Looks like one of those other choices for dancing fun may have been the Paw Paw Dance Club. Probably born in the early '50s, it nicely filled the void left after *Salvage* disappeared below the waves. Like-minded couples got together and invited friends, and membership grew. In the beginning there were: Joyce and Chuck Sage from the U.S.S. Salvage building crew; Ed and Peg Brennan, Dad's schoolmates from Paw Paw High School years; Bill and Katie Woodman, local farm kids; and Horace Adams, village attorney and his wife Mary who were longtime Paw Paw residents and in on the fun from the start. I would suppose that Bill and June Warner, Bob and Jackie Harrison, and Jon and Betty Woodman were early members, too. Lucky for me, Joyce Sage is still with us at this writing and told me she thought it didn't take long to grow the crowd to about twenty-five couples. But when I called Mary Adams to ask about her memories, she said there were at least fifty couples after just a few years.

The Club got together five times a year on Saturday nights in the Old Walnut Room above Sportsman's Bar and Grill on Main Street. With that many people in membership, I think that place must have been one rowdy scene. They were mostly veterans and their spouses. They enjoyed the Big Band sounds and swing style dancing, and Barb and Jim Jennings never missed one of these parties. The evening always started out at about 8 p.m. with drinks in our living room for a few of their special friends and then off to dance with the big crowd until the wee hours next morning. The ladies put on their most sparkly outfits, the men wore their best suits and ties and everyone smelled really good. By 1960 when Kay went away to Kalamazoo College, I was old enough to have a friend stay with me on those nights without adult supervision. This was big stuff for me and my pals. We looked forward to Dance Club nights for weeks beforehand. Not that there was much mischief-making of any kind, but there was Saturday Night at the Movies to be watched, popcorn and other treats to be shared, and just a certain sense of independence to be relished for a few hours. You see, The Paw Paw Dance Club had far-reaching, though probably incidental, effects even for those of us who never ventured to the Walnut Room.

The original intention of the Club was to keep costs low and still enjoy some high-style fun. Nobody had much money, so it was a BYO affair. A committee was appointed for each dance to plan themes, make sandwiches, decorate and then clean up afterwards. Mary told me that sometimes Earl Flick played his piano and brought a drummer and maybe one other musician with him. Joyce said at other times, Chuck set up his powerful sound system and played disc jockey with his 78-rpm big band record collection. That made it really neat because everyone got to dance to original orchestra sounds. Whatever the case, Joyce stressed to me, for the purpose of writing this account and for all to know for sure, they always had a "really good time."

It takes spirit and dedication to make something like this happen and to keep it going. Mary thinks much of the success was due to Stan and Jean Phillips. Stan was the studio art teacher in the Paw Paw school system for a while and liberally applied his creativity when it came to Dance Club ventures. She said Stan's Halloween costumes were always the most distinctive and challenged everyone else to use as much imagination as they could to come up with unusual and fun ideas, too.

Of course News Year's Eve was the fanciest dance party. The guys turned out in tuxedos and the gals sometimes in long formal gowns, if they had one. I never saw Mom and Dad do that, but Kay assures me it did happen. I was just too little then to know. But what I do remember was the prologue to these events when I got old enough to notice. I usually planted myself on Mom and Dad's double bed and watched every aspect of the preparation. Formal evening attire was not the norm in town, at least not for my folks. So this was an exciting change of scene to one impressionable adolescent onlooker. All showered and freshly shaved, Dad pulled out a starched white dress shirt with French cuffs just back from the laundry and selected one of his few neckties that Kay and I probably gave him for Father's Day. He fastened his top button, turned up the collar, threw the tie around his neck and began weaving his magic to produce a perfectly balanced Windsor knot. I think he took pride in those knots. Maybe he learned how to tie these in the Air Corps. Whatever the case, I remember it well because he passed this skill on to me when

I needed it for my red coated band uniform some years later. As a finishing touch, there were the cufflinks. He had a few sets and carefully selected which ones to use that night. I remember I was so impressed at how he placed them in their proper position using only one hand.

Mom's preparation of course was a bit more intricate than Dad's. Hair and makeup were tended to while she was seated at her dressing table with mirrors and lamps on all sides. Her outfits were fancy and she finished them off with accessories. Earrings, necklace, sparkly evening bag and gloves were required, of course. The result: they were picture perfect, wafting aftershave and flowery perfume, and ready for the evening. What a show!

I think Dance Club flourished for at least fifteen years, though I lost track when I went off to school in '66. Mary says people started to fall away after the committee work got farmed out to caterers and other services. Esprit de corps dwindled. Then, of course, the Andrews Sisters' "Boogie Woogie Bugle Boy," Tommy Dorsey's "Once In A While," and Glenn Miller's "In the Mood" yielded to Presley's "You Ain't Nothin' but a Hound Dog" and the Beatles' "I Want to Hold Your Hand." Rock music took hold and then, certainly, our elders developed over the years inevitable maladies that required a slower pace and not so much dancing.

There was considerable drinking and smoking going on at those events too and these led to problems later on for some of our heros. But that's the stuff for stories of a different sort. The big take-away here is that the group continued for as long as it did because those folks formed a special bond as brothers and sisters when they united against evil oppression. As I look back on it now, it's plain to see that the U.S.S. Salvage and that Dance Club reinforced their bond and actually served as a therapeutic balm against lingering invisible wounds from the war. The Dance Club became a big family, doing what families do—loving, supporting, caring, laughing, grieving and playing together. It was a kinship that even carried over to their kids. Another incidental benefit was that it gave me and my pals dozens of surrogate aunts and uncles all over town. Those people looked out for us during our most important and vulnerable formative years and left lessons for healthy, harmonious living. As I think about it, those lessons could have come straight out of their military manuals for proper decorum:

Bragging is not allowed.
Complaining gets you nowhere.
If something isn't right, come together, set goals, do your part and share in the outcome.
"One for all and all for one" is the rule.
Love and respect your brothers and sisters.
Live with joy and grace in precious Liberty.

Author Mart, enjoying the view in 2000

# 'And the Old Shall be New Again'
## (Ecclesiastes 1:9, Mart's Version)

My local school system in Western Massachusetts is hiring thirty-four new art and music teachers for the coming fall semester. Every student in every citywide public school will benefit. The announcement said that these subjects "lend variety to the educational experience" and "allow children to become more well-rounded and intellectually versatile." Well, I am pleased. This is a resurrection of delightful classes I remember from my own early school days. You see? If you wait long enough, the old ways will be new again! It certainly happens with fashion and food! Why not education? But I can't help wondering: Why is this happening now? And: Why was this instruction excluded for so long? Was it about money? Were politics involved? If so, what's the story? I suppose the answers are complex. Actually, the state of affairs that demanded their *inclusion* in the first place was complex. It was a time that shaped my life at Paw Paw Elementary School. And by the way, it seems my school curriculum was an exception to the ancient scriptural idiom cited above. The public school experience in those days was something distinctly new—never done on a large scale ever before—definitely unique—not recycled—absolutely special! I don't think a lot of people know that. So read on!

The '50s ushered in a brand new age. The Allies had prevailed. Vets were back home. Families were reunited and kids were coming out of the woodwork with an unprecedented birth rate. Mom and Dad were building a life from the ground up, hopeful that a peaceful world, free from tyranny and hate, would dominate their future. Part of that hope showed up as an embrace of progressive new trends in education for their two daughters. The public school system at least partially banished "Old School" English- and German-based teaching methods used on this side of the Atlantic since before our nation's founding. This was big (!!!), first of all, because people normally don't like change. But beside that, postwar patriots were ready for an education system distinctively American, designed by Americans and relevant to American values: multicultural, pluralistic, liberty-for-all. As it turned out, the timing was just right. An "active learning" model, American in character, designed by American progressive philosopher and educator John Dewey, was ready and waiting to go to work.

My sister Kay was a war baby, born in 1941, and started school in '46 at the big building on Michigan Avenue. New teaching methods based on Dewey's model were integrated in the school curriculum by then and well established by the time I was ready for first grade some seven years later. But there was one big difference between Kay's school days and mine: the venue. I was among the "boomers," the huge influx of children who taxed existing infrastructures after World War II. The 1950 and 1960 census statistics for Paw Paw show about a 25% population increase for each of those decades. By 1960 and a few years thereafter, when the boom was on the decline, boom babies numbered well over seventy-six million nationwide or roughly forty percent of the 1965 national population! Boards of education across the country built new schools to handle the crowds and the board in Paw Paw, Michigan was no exception. So in 1954, we little ones got special treatment in the form of a brand new school building we could call our own on Cedar Street.

Even the building design was influenced by Dewey's ideas. It was child centered, and sleek in style with everything we needed right there and on one floor: self-contained classrooms with hot and cold running water, lavatories, plenty of group work areas away from our desks, and big windows that let in lots of natural light and let us look out on the world around us. There was a library down the long hallway and a gymnasium area that doubled as auditorium, lunchroom, or whatever else that needed a big space. The lawns were large and very green, and were used for maypole dancing in the springtime and maybe for story telling on the grass, if the weather was right and teachers agreeable.

Architect's rendering of Cedar Street School as it appeared in the 1953 edition of the *Wappaw,* Paw Paw High School yearbook. Reprinted here with permission from Paw Paw Public School Administration. This is how I remember it though without trees.

Our teachers were dedicated, energetic, credentialed, certified, and on their toes. Louise Myers, Elizabeth McQuigg, and Margaret Ford, to name a few, reached way down into their bag of tricks  to set up active learning exercises, also known as "learning by doing," all fashioned to conform with Dewey's framework. It was demanding work, much more so than simple lectures, rote memorization and regurgitation, and I think probably a lot more fun for our teachers and for us. They used what today could be called a "balanced approach." It included traditional instruction in the three R's for sure. But then it directed us to go beyond. It forced us to collaborate with our peers. It required knowledge application through problem solving and put us in direct communication with people in the Paw Paw community and our whole Southwest Michigan region. The intent was to help us make connections between what we learned in class and how that knowledge makes a difference in the world around us.

Field trips were commonplace. Twenty little kids climbed into a bus and traveled to an unfamiliar place. In one case it was Maple City Dairy right in town. In another, it was the Post Cereals plant in Battle Creek. We learned where our morning milk and Post Toasties came from and how they were made. Twenty little kids with short, short, short attention spans! We needed encouragement, affirmation and guidance—sometimes all at once. How did those women (mostly women) keep their sanity? The truth is that they managed because they were super skilled and professionally equipped in planning for applied learning. They knew exactly how to bring on what educators call "Aha! Moments." Aha!, when eyes open wide, faces light up and smiles appear. Aha! is the proof that understanding is present. It's a magical moment—when everything gels. Aha! is the big payoff. The trouble proves worth the effort and aha! moments inspire some people to choose teaching as a career. But then I suppose our teachers also managed well because a team of three itinerant specialists delivered lessons in art, music and physical education for us on a weekly basis.

These traveling educators enriched our experience and gave our homeroom teachers plenty more inspiration to build on. They also allowed some reprieve from an otherwise hectic pace, which was then wisely used for planning even more active learning exercises.

A jovial fellow named Walter Wagner taught the studio art lessons. He wore an artist's smock and pushed his cart loaded with supplies through our doorway as we watched and waited to see what kind of creations were in store. The one I recall best was a lesson in making puppet heads out of papier mache wrapped around light bulbs. Once the pasty paper wrapping was dry and very carefully opened with a razor blade by Mr. Wagner, the light bulb was removed. Its casing was closed back up with more gooey paper, dried again, and finally the product was ready for painting on its surface whatever kind of funny face we wanted. I suppose we attached some simple kind of garment for it with sleeves and hands to complete the doll and then used it to act out a puppet show. This was a thrill! I followed Mr. Wagner's direction and I made it happen! The lesson was about goal setting, making uncommon use of common items and tending to simple sequential steps to complete a complex task. It was learning by doing that could be applied in other settings for other purposes. I was triumphant and empowered!

Mrs. Beals (Edith Beals) arrived weekly too. Beals was a proper sort, always tastefully dressed with lace hankie tucked up under one sleeve. She reminded me of my grandmother McKinstry—quite the grand lady—except that Beals made her entrance at the back end of her standard-sized upright piano. She came to teach music and yes, she pushed that piano up and down the hallway under her own steam. I suppose the exercise kept her in good condition over all those years. But in my mind it was an odd circumstance for a lady of her sophistication. "How could this be?," I thought. A grand lady pushing this huge piece of equipment down the hall as if she were a stagehand? It didn't fit with my ideas about what was appropriate, one of the first times I remember recognizing maybe I had it all wrong. Beals was classy for sure but definitely no shrinking violet. Rather, she was a very sturdy woman in both strength and spirit. I learned from Beals that women could be many things all at the same time and that is exactly what we learned to do under her direction...many things all at one time.

Mrs. Beals taught from an American songbook. We all had copies kept in our desks, and I recall that music class, at least for me, was not necessarily a fun time. Beals insisted we count out rhythms by tapping the appropriate values for each note in the book using our index finger and a stiff up-and-down chopping motion from the elbow done in unison. As I think about it now, this scene might have resembled some kind of Nazi drill...maybe a carry over from old-school German militaristic methods? Well, to Beals, learning to count was paramount, old school or not, and once a rhythm was learned, she used the piano to illustrate the melodies. When the pitch pipe came out of her pocket, that was our cue to mimic the tone she produced as a starting place and we sang lyrics to the melody and counted out the values as we went. Yes, this was just as complex as completing the art projects, except that Beals was asking us to manage the complexity not step by step but rather all at once! And we didn't always get it right! It was a struggle.    Yet to this day, I am thankful that Edith Beals persevered.  Years later, I excelled as a team player on my clarinet in the high school band and in singing groups, reading the score, making the music and marching or singing all at the same time because Edith Beals taught me how.  Of course, the songs we learned from Mrs. Beals were standbys at school assemblies and elsewhere—another connection with the world around us.

The third itinerant was Miss Spaulding, our gym teacher. Marion Spaulding did her best to see that we tested our strength, endurance and agility to the limit.   There were lessons in rope climbing, acrobatics, ball sports of all kinds, relays and of course, racing.  Most of the time P.E. was held outdoors, where there was fresh air and a lot of space to move, another Dewey directive.  Our playground was huge, with expansive sandy fields for kickball and other games that required running.  The area immediately adjacent to the building and away from the sand was an asphalt surface reserved for hopscotch, jump rope, or shooting hoops, and Spaulding used it all.  Looking back on it, I can now appreciate the value of teamwork,  knowing the rules of the game, esprit de corps, and physical fitness intrinsic in all these games.  That's what we learned from Miss Spaulding.  But I must admit that I was not an aspiring athlete.  Natural science was a stronger calling for me, and I was distracted during gym class by the forbidden creek that separated the ball fields from the wetland areas beyond.  This was a place where we were not supposed to go unaccompanied, and of course that made it all the more alluring.  There was wildlife in that creek:  pollywogs, frogs, turtles, and I suppose maybe even snakes. How could I keep my mind on team sports when I knew the tadpoles were swimming so close by?

I think the ultimate of all learning-by-doing exercises in elementary school happened during the week I spent at Fifth Grade Winter Camp.  A lot of  shenanigans with my two closest pals at that time came to light and stand out because of this exceptional learning and growth-filled experience.  It was a tradition.  The fifth graders went to winter camp for five days every February.  This was a rite of passage in our school and was anticipated impatiently from third grade on.  "Gee, I can't wait to go to camp" was the refrain.  There was much snow on the ground and several inches of ice on the lake. I borrowed a sleeping bag, took along Dad's olive drab wool Army blanket and slept in a barracks-like dormitory building. The boys' bunks were in a large room on one side of the building and the girls' in an equally large room on the other side. Our bonded threesome, then at age ten, was me, Jeannie Ranson and Debbie Clair. We were inseparable and into all kinds of funny business. Life was one curiosity after another and we relished it all.

Our fifth grade teacher was an up-and-comer named Larry DeVogd, a good- natured, athletic type fellow absolutely dedicated to kids and education. DeVogd was destined to rise through the ranks to principal and then other high levels of the Michigan educational system. But for a short time, he was ours along with a student teacher with spirit to match Larry's, and we were all set for adventure.

There were forty or fifty ten-year-olds, off without parental supervision, charged with keeping track of our own belongings, following some new rules for campers, cooperating with peers, and finding ways to solve problems. With our teachers as guides, the week was filled with plenty of survival and team-building challenges, one of which was the notorious "drop off hike." We were broken into small groups and Debbie, Jeannie and I were deliberately not placed together. They loaded us onto the bus and each group got dropped off in parts unknown at some distance from camp. Each group had one adult, a map, a compass, and the task of finding our way back before dinner. It was kind of scary, we had our doubts, and it took several hours, but we made it. Imagine our sense of relief and accomplishment. We met the challenge and self-esteem went up at least one or two notches!

The next task was an early-morning venture out on the ice-covered lake to cook breakfast over a bonfire. The smoke was intense and there was much coughing and many teary eyes as we tried to get as close to the flames as safely possible to keep warm. The food was not memorable, since most of it didn't get cooked through, and we looked forward to lunch in the mess hall because we didn't get much to eat that morning. Was it a failed venture? Maybe. Maybe not. We certainly had a new appreciation for our warm beds and predictable meal schedules thereafter.

Then there were the dreaded gang showers. We heard from the sixth graders that we were expected to shower together all at once, and this prospect was anticipated with some trepidation. Bobbie, the counselor assigned to the girls' dorm, assured us that there was really no reason to be excessively modest about our various stages of budding femininity. She said that we were all basically the same. We needn't be self-conscious. Well, this was a first for me. I had never been naked with anyone other than my mother and I *was* self-conscious, at least until I stepped into the shower to find Debbie squealing and laughing while sliding across the soapy shower floor on her bare bottom. Of course then we all wanted to join in and there was absolutely no problem going "au naturel" with the crowd at any time thereafter. A lot of bonding, maturation and self-confidence emerged during those five days. I had stories to tell and camp songs to share with Mom and Dad over dinner when I got home. They were happy and proud as they listened and laughed along with me at the learning and growth that came out of my five days at Fifth Grade Winter Camp.

Yes, Mom and Dad were pleased. They never once suggested their tax dollars were ill spent on frivolities at school. Not once did they question our teachers' judgment. Never once did Mom miss a parent/teacher conference. Mom was a teacher herself and carefully discerning when it came to our education. Dad trusted Mom's judgement on quality, but he too was always interested and involved in our schooling. Mom and Dad were in sync with Paw Paw's public school system. It was turning out the level of achievement they expected. Of course Kay and I didn't know any alternative. We assumed it was as it should be: forever and ever, amen. This was the Paw Paw public school way for years and years for us and for the kids who followed until…the presidential campaign of 1980 changed everything.

Education was a hot-button issue. Some Americans were unsettled about progressive trends in public school teaching methods. Old-school approaches originated with the earliest Protestant settlers in the new world: Dutch Reformed, Anglican, Lutheran, etc. Church-related schools within each denomination reflected distinctive religious doctrines. Then, after the Revolution, Catholic schools also became a major force in the mix.

By contrast, the progressive movement of the late 1800's into the early 20th century proposed clear separation between church and state. The progressive child-centered model focused primarily on the development of each child's innate natural character qualities and encouraged growth according to these individual differences. Guidelines for moral development emphasized the "Golden Rule" as our code for acceptable social behavior. But references to the Deity were limited to daily recitals of the Pledge of Allegiance and maybe a few lyrics for Christmas or Thanksgiving songs. The result of all this was that many traditionalists took exception to these types of priorities and omissions.

Ronald Reagan capitalized on the discontent and promised to abolish the Department of Education. This would at least symbolically put more emphasis on states' rights and recognize the power of local school boards in governing their own education systems. Then, after Reagan was elected, the new Secretary of Education, Terrel Bell, went further by pulling together a special commission to scrutinize public school achievement scores. The result was the notorious *A Nation at Risk* report. It came out in 1983 and claimed that academic achievement among American public school children was lagging way behind their international peer groups. It contained hyperbolic claims like, "the educational foundations of our society are presently being eroded by a 'Rising Tide of Mediocrity'." (p.5). "Johnny can't read!" appeared in press headlines, and Reagan vowed to get tough on education. Shocked and outraged citizens were behind him 100%, and Reagan's approval polls climbed. Plans were put in place to raise test scores for reading and math skills by increasing time spent on those subjects and completely eliminating time for previously popular learning by doing. A push toward "back-to-basics" ensued. The "old" was new again and the change has remained a political bone of contention for forty years.

Most people know about the course of events as described above and the sad state of affairs we have now because of school reform disagreements. But most do not know that the '80s strategies for improving test scores had questionable cause. Terrel Bell's commission, deliberately or not, left expert counsel out of the decision making mix. Commission membership included only one teacher and zero educational scholars. But even more alarming is that commission conclusions on student acheivement levels may have been based on faulty data interpretation that conveniently supported Reagan's political agenda. It certainly appeared that way when a challenge study done by Sandia National Laboratories in 1990 reanalyzed the same data. Sandia revealed an entirely different story. That is, all subgroup achievement scores had actually increased, not decreased. Wow! In statistics, this mathematical anomaly is known as "Simpson's Paradox" and makes all the difference when sorting out meaning for multiple group test scores. Sadly, most people don't know about Sandia. It went unacknowledged by our government and even the press. In the end, our nation didn't have enough information to know that Reagan's popular education reform movement had a doubtful basis. This discovery makes me very sad. The push for back-to-basics, more testing and alternative school choices as remedies for low scores may have been quite unnecessary from the beginning. The result was that teachers were forced into roles and practices they knew were less productive and students missed out on what could have been valuable learning experiences. It appears that many professional careers were senselessly disrupted and student growth shortchanged.

Despite this unfortunate historical morass, there is a glimmer of hope for the future. A few successful teaching methods from that time may be gaining favor once more. At least it seems that way in view of the thirty-four new art and music teachers recently hired by my local school system. From the above description I think it is clear that making assumptions can be a dangerous thing. Yet it's a good bet our school board here in Western Massachusetts is aware that learning in the arts improves skills for critical thinking, creative problem solving, effective communication, and comfort in collaboration. All of these are more commonly known today as "skills for the 21st century". Isn't it interesting how the same higher-order thinking and performance goals the boomers learned so long ago are now called skills for the 21st century? Looks like Dewey was waaaay...ahead of his time!!! Learning by doing lasted a good long while before its disruption. But now, after a 40-year hiatus, some neglected pieces of Dewey's plan have been restored for at least a few New England boomer grandchildren. Maybe for them and their progeny, today's reincarnation of the old as new again will last for a good long while, too. I hope so.

Some of my classmates from elementary school days at John Fleming's birthday party. Maybe we were seven or eight, circa 1958. Foreground: Shelly Rupert and Gary Pardike. Second row: Mary Jane Dillon, me, John, Judy Mesick. Third row: Freddy Shafer, Bobby Cramer, Sherry Sage behind me, Wendy Ball making a face. Background: Jeri Cole, Donny Hall and David Honeycut.

# 'Time Travel'

What do you think about traveling back in time...to make up for some mistake made long ago? Or maybe to see some place, some event or some person in history? If you could, would you do it? It might be exciting. Or it could be startling or disappointing, or take the magic out of childhood memories. So, no, I think at least for now I'll accept my recollections just the way they are.

Some of the most delightful of those memories are from the '50s when I was about eight or nine. We lived on North Van Buren Street and I rode my kid's sized bike around that part of town all the time checking out who was doing what. One day I passed by the gate at Tyler Field, our school athletic complex, and noticed a crowd at the baseball diamond. I looked in and saw kids lined up, waiting with autograph books in hand to get a signature from hometown celebrity Charlie Maxwell, the Detroit Tigers' Sunday home run hitter. Maxwell was actually a Lawton native, but he made his home in Paw Paw and I knew him from watching the Tigers play on TV every Sunday afternoon. He was known to the sportscasters as "Ol Paw Paw," and we folks at home loved it.

Well, never one to pass up an opportunity, I was compelled to join in even if I didn't have the right equipment. No pen, no autograph book, but still determined, I bummed a scrap of paper from someone and then cornered a lady totally unknown to me standing nearby and asked if she had something I could use for writing. She dug down deep in her purse and produced the stubbiest of pencils you can imagine. But it worked. I got his signature and raced home to show Mom. I don't really think it was the autograph that thrilled me so. Rather, it was the fact I happened upon this neat scene and got to take part. I guess the strength of that memory is partly due to my temperament at the time: insistent that I must not miss out. Then there was all the excitement of the crowd, and I was caught up in it. The pay-off was in the pride of being resourceful on the spot and in sharing it all with Mom so she could be proud too. No, I wouldn't want to take a chance on spoiling *that* sweet reminiscence.

Tyler Field was a major meeting place in town and the catalyst for a bunch of neat memories because of it. The baseball diamond was at the extreme north end, a football field ringed by a quarter-mile cinder surface running track in the center and tennis courts to the south. Tyler Field was where Dad ran hurdles and scored touchdowns in the '30s. It was where starstruck kids like me got up close with big league players. A huge stage was constructed in the outfield during Paw Paw's Village Centennial Celebration in 1959 when I was eleven. Kay and I and our friends lobbed tennis balls around the courts on summer afternoons. And this is where I marched with the high school band when we practiced our halftime shows on Tuesday nights directed by Marshall Myers. It was not just for athletes. Non-athletes joined in too. There were all kinds of events that shaped the lives of Paw Paw folks for generations.

I learned from Butch Hindenach's *Tales, Legends, Myths and Notable Citizens of Paw Paw* that Tyler Field was built in stages. The baseball diamond came first in 1908. Teddy Roosevelt was President then. Henry Ford was making his Model T on assembly lines in Dearborn, and Maple Lake, on the west side of town, was only one year old. A new ball field was needed to replace the one that got flooded when the lake was made. So Paw Paw's school board purchased a parcel for that purpose. The rest of the land was gifted by Mrs. George Tyler around 1923, when the football field with running track was installed. Then ten years after that, tennis courts were added with a handsome stone wall erected on the perimeter of the complex.

These events happened way before my time. But my personal memories of Tyler Field, including the day I came upon

Charlie Maxwell, are indeed emotionally-charged happenings. There was excitement, challenge, and then victory, all the stuff that makes lasting impressions.

My most meaningful memories at Tyler center around high school band halftime shows. In the early '60s, I stepped off from the west endzone with my bandmates in our red and black uniforms to give the crowd something flashy to look at and listen to. All of our shows had a theme, and one in particular sticks in my mind because it required an impersonation of the latest rock idol, Elvis Presley. And who do you think was picked to play this role? Yes, I was an Elvis mimic, entertaining my friends at parties with my impressions of the teenage heartthrob. The word got out about this and band director Marshall Myers asked me to audition. I wasn't sure what I was getting myself into, but I agreed and he liked what he saw. So I borrowed a pair of Levis from my neighbor Bob Brennan, greased and combed my hair into a pompadour, and ran out onto the field on cue for the show. I swivelled my hips, shook my legs and engaged in other Presley-style gyrations as the band played some rock and roll sounds behind me. I really don't remember much. It was my first time playing solo to a crowd of that size, and I think I was just trying to get through it without fainting.

I suppose Mom and Dad were there to witness the thing and lend support. They usually showed up whenever I was on stage. And for sure, this was another emotion-packed episode. I was putting myself out there for everyone to see, all duded up like Elvis with my family watching me. I could have fallen on my face. The stakes were high and I was taking a risk. It was important not to fail both for me and for the people depending on me. But the crowd seemed to like it. So once again I was triumphant at Tyler Field. No wonder I have a soft spot for the place. But still, I have no wish to return to those times. It worked just fine and I'll leave it as it is.

I wonder though if Dad, while watching my antics, reflected back on his own history at Tyler? If he did, what might have come to his mind? It's hard to know. I have written elsewhere that Dad was a mild-mannered, modest fellow and never one to blow his own horn about anything. So Kay and I never knew about his triumphs at Tyler Field to say nothing of his thoughts about them. But in 1999, a full forty years after Dad was gone, Aunt Irene found a small box tucked away on a shelf in our grandmother's garage. It was filled with ribbons and medals Dad won at track meets. Some date back to '28 and '29, when he was 13 or 14 years old. Irene said Dad was a standout athlete and Pa (our grandfather) never missed a meet or football game. But as far as I knew none of those awards were displayed anywhere in our grandparents' home.

I told Coach Falan about the box and learned from him that indeed, Dad was a star in track and football at Paw Paw High School. High and low hurdles were his specialty and he set the Tyler Field record for both events in 1934. Most of his speeds have been reset many times over since those days. Yet one distinction remains. At the state meet that same year, he finished first in the 220-yard low hurdles with a speed of 26.8 seconds. That distance was retired after his run, so he remains the final challenger to win this distance for all time.

Yes, he was fast! Twenty-six and eight-tenths of a second translates to 16.79 miles per hour, and it looks like this same speed showed up on the gridiron, too. He was known by teammates as a "swivel-hip/slasher"-type runner, a player who can make quick changes in direction and accelerate quickly through openings in the opposing team's line. These traits must have given him an edge during the 1931 season opener against Plainwell, when he ran 80 yards on an interception to score in the 20-0 win. His teammates said he always gave 100%, and that causes me to wonder if he was running over 16 miles per hour on *that* day, too. I found out about the interception touchdown 65 years after the fact only by way of an old newspaper clipping. Again, he never said anything. Kay and I had no idea.

Why was he so quiet about this? Was some deep, dark secret involved? Now, all these years later, I think I finally figured it out. Dad's sports history and good grades in school were a source of pride for the family, and his future had bright prospects because of it. Both Michigan State and Michigan sought him out for the fall of '34. He chose Michigan, and Kay and I agree he might have studied engineering or history or politics. But he never got to Ann Arbor.  Aunt Irene told us he caught malaria on a pre-college trip to Mexico with his pals.  His illness was severe and the family feared for the worst.  Treatments were limited then and recovery was slow, and when it did come, his strength was gone.  The family struggled during the Great Depression.  Tuition costs at Michigan were beyond reach without his scholarship.    Dad's chance for higher education was gone, too.  It must have been a devastating blow for him and the family.  My guess is that the disappointment and frustration may have made his ribbons and medals just too painful to have around, so Gommie (grandma) and Pa (grandpa) probably tucked them away out of sight.  Recurring secondary symptoms related to the illness were most likely rude reminders of his loss too, and perhaps a source of self-blame for making that trip in the first place.  But on the other side, I think the experience probably strengthened his resolve to see that his kids made wiser choices and were never deprived in this way.  Both Mom and Dad, though for very different reasons, agreed their girls absolutely must become college-educated women.  We got this message loudly, clearly and repeatedly from very early childhood, and that is the major reason why it came to be.

Dad ran track and played football for all four years in high school.  He was captain of the ball team as a senior and, as of 1999, Coach Falan told me Dad ranked #12 in individual scoring, with 92 points for Paw Paw High School.  He was on the All-South Western Michigan Honor Football Team and won State All Star Honors in 1933.  Our mild-mannered Dad was a star athlete and a good bit of his scoring happened right at Tyler Field.  These facts I learned about Dad are super emotionally-charged stuff---a side of my Dad I never knew, a new part of my own identity, where I came from, my DNA.  On top of that, I'm sad about his losses, joyous and proud at his triumphs and thankful I finally get to celebrate these things even now, almost ninety years after the fact.

Of course, the celebration would be sweeter with him still here so we could share the memories.  He could tell me how fast he was running and how loud maybe the crowd was cheering. But to be there and see Dad as a teen, in tip-top condition on the field…running at full speed for his 80-yard score…clearing the hurdles over 220 yards on the cinder track… and Pa beaming proudly from the sidelines…to see that, well, let's just say I'm reconsidering my rule against time travel.

Four year letter man,
 James Jennings

Paw Paw High School 1934 (the year the stone wall was built at Tyler Field)

# 'Red Coats'

The TV host said, "And here comes the Red Coated Paw Paw High School Marching Band." It must have been Thanksgiving and maybe this was a televised parade from Detroit. The details are lost. All I recall is the message about red coats. I was only six or seven years old but I knew right then I wanted to wear the red coat and march in a parade like that one with the band. Wouldn't that be cool? And it *was* cool.

The road to make it happen started in the fourth grade. Band director Marshall Myers traveled over to the elementary school on Cedar Street every week. He instructed aspiring bandsmen, ages nine to twelve, to read a score, learn elementary fingerings and work our lips and tongues so to produce sound from our horns of various kinds. I chose the clarinet. Mom and Dad bought one second hand for me. Thirty dollars sticks in my mind and even that seems like a lot of money for a used horn in those days. So the cost may have been less. Johnny Fleming had his grandfather's vintage trumpet. Other kids had flutes, trombones and cornets. We all got specific instructions and went home to practice.

A lot of squeaking came out of my room after school and sometimes Mom and Dad put a limit on when and for how long I could practice. But eventually identifiable tunes emerged, my fingers moved across the keys with greater ease and squeaky reeds became a thing of the past. I loved it! Especially the low tones. Clarinets sound warm and sensual in the lower octaves and I liked those passages the most. I think I also felt a sense of personal power when I played and mastered a passage. I worked and worked to get it just right—over and over and over. That's when I usually heard a knock at the door. It was Mom: "Mart, have you finished your Latin homework yet?" The answer was usually , "Uh, no," and then my practice session ended for the night.

For seven or eight years, that clarinet and the band were major forces in my life, parts of my identity. I learned to remove and replace my own worn-out key pads and tighten tiny screws to keep that horn in tip-top shape. The leather handle on its case finally gave way after years of lugging the thing back and forth from home to school. But a length of rope worked just fine for the same purpose. No problem. Fourth-, fifth- and sixth-grade practice was the prelude to Junior High Band membership where we appeared in annual concerts as a warm-up act before the Senior High Concert Band showed up as the main event. We didn't have fancy uniforms then, but we did have special yellow sweatshirts with "Paw Paw Junior High School Band" across the front. We wore them for concerts and marching in Homecoming and Memorial Day parades. The upperclassmen helped us put them on and made sure we didn't look sloppy. That was a clear message about uniforms for band—we had to look sharp.

When the day finally came in the fall of 1962, in my freshman year, I was fitted out in red coat, red cap and black trousers. I recall clearly what it was like. Myers waited outside the uniform storage room. A female upper-class bandsman helped me select and try on uniform items that fit. Then my appearance was inspected and approved by Myers before I could take the items home. It was like a military detail. And the uniforms were military in style. We wore "peaked"-style caps...short black visor, black band, flat red top, no plume. Our coats were single-breasted, brass-buttoned U.S. Army dress uniform-style jackets that fell below the hip. There was a coiled black braid at the left shoulder finished with brass finial, black piping at the cuffs, black belt at the waist with brass military-style buckle, no gloves. Trousers were black with red stripe down the side. We were responsible for our own black shoes, socks and tie to be worn with a long-sleeve white collared shirt. This was the uniform I saw in that Thanksgiving Day parade and was in force at PPHS from 1952 through 1967.

My entire band experience in school overlapped perfectly with the life of the red coat at Paw Paw and the early career of Marshall Myers, the only band director I ever knew. I believe Myers arrived at Paw Paw as Instrumental Music Director in 1954 or 1955, and I took up the clarinet in 1957 as he was laying the foundation for a top-performing high school marching and concert band. I understand that some in the band took exception to Myers' regimented style. But to me, Myers seemed totally dedicated to music education. His instruction was specific and clear. I never had a question about what he expected of me. And I never questioned his sensitivity and caring as a teacher. It was easy and natural to work like crazy to please him.

Wearing the red coat was an honor and a responsibility. We were representing our school and our peers took pride in the band. We wanted to live up to that. Expectations were clear in the lessons Myers taught us. We functioned as a team. Everyone had their part to play. One for all and all for one...that's the way it was.

The word *hustle* took on significant meaning from the earliest years in band. There was no dawdling when risers, folding chairs and music stands needed transport and arrangement. We "hustled" too, about being in the right spot at just the right time when it came to field formations or "dress right" line ups for parades. No one was out of step for long. Our peers enforced the code. Everyone kept in step to look sharp.

All this came about by way of practice with a capital "P." Practicing the music we played of course required solo sessions at home. Then there were at least a couple of rehearsals per week during class time with the entire band. One thing that kept us on our toes about solo practicing was the unannounced section tryout. If a given section did not sound clear, concert practice came to a screeching halt and each player in that row endured a challenge to play the troubling passage solo before the entire band. When we were not prepared, it was a very humbling experience. Everyone in the room witnessed our failure to learn the score. I think I was caught off guard a couple of times this way and got demoted. But it worked the other way for me too. There was once a very demanding passage for second chair clarinet in Richard Rogers' "Victory at Sea" and Myers stopped directing, turned to my row and demanded each of us, one by one, demonstrate our skill. Well...this just happened to be a passage I was using at home for warm-ups and was quite good at it. In fact, there were audible "oohs and aahs" in the room as I played and then was promoted to first row, third seat. I went from second tier, top seat to first tier, bottom seat followed at first with pride and then with a bit of personal confusion. The promotion brought peer admiration but then demanded mastery of a more difficult score. Did I really want this? The lesson learned here is classic: diligence and hard work are usually rewarded with more and even harder work. So "Be careful what you ask for." It's so true! And, like me, you might not even know that you are asking!

I think my first year with the high school marching band was also the first year that Myers changed formation styles at halftime shows. He went to a band director's conference somewhere and came back with all kinds of fancy ideas for using geometric patterns in our programs. In the old days before my time in band, the bandsmen used a "scramble" style for changing formations on the field. Each person left his or her position and marched or ran to a designated spot for the next part of the show. To the casual observer, it looked like a "scramble," not very interesting and kind of messy. But when I arrived as a freshman, Myers was working out elaborate movements so our formations evolved one into another and folks in the bleachers witnessed a kind of morphing effect as patterns changed. No scrambling. It was neat and the beginning of a new era in marching band field-formation history at Paw Paw.

Our halftime shows told a story and each one of us had a part to play. One show had a patriotic theme, with the band marching in pinwheel formations of some kind. Carbon dioxide fire extinguishers at the end of pinwheel spokes blasted out white streams as we blared strains of George M. Cohan's "You're a Grand Old Flag" across the field. In a jazzy adaptation of "Seeing Nellie Home," entitled "Aunt Dinah's Quilting Party Hop," squares of bandsmen representing quilting blocks moved up and down and in and out of the yard lines as we played. I suppose these moves could never hold a candle to the fancy shows of today's marching bands, yet our crowds at home loved them and we took those shows to competitions. I don't know if we won anything, but we sure had a great time strutting our stuff.

Practice was never more prominent than at band camp. For one week each summer we packed up our gear and headed for the Van Buren County Youth Camp on Great Bear Lake. Now, for the non-bandsman reading this piece, it's important that I describe here in some detail just what band camp involved. It was not just being at the lake and once in a while playing a tune or two. No. Instead, Myers had his work cut out for him.

Our ages ranged from fourteen to eighteen and we were a co-educational group. Adolescent hormones were most likely raging. And we were away from parental supervision for a week. But Myers handled it in his usual no-nonsense-style. We functioned with military precision. Eight of us were assigned by gender to each cabin, with one upperclassman per cabin in charge. Reveille got us up in the morning, then down the path to the bathhouse for a shower, back to the cabin to dress and then "hustled" down lakeside for flag raising. Next was breakfast in the lodge, where we served and cleared our own tables. After all meals we usually sang or chanted some form of thanks to our cook, Pearl Fisk, who took care of nutritional needs for the week. Then we were off to clean up in and around our cabins before inspection. Yes, we were expected to keep our quarters and grounds spotless and then endure intense scrutiny about it by camp staff. We all lined up outside our respective cabins for this detail and, once approval was granted, piled onto the bus to spend the next one to two hours in marching practice on a nearby field Myers called "the upper 40." There was about one-half-hour of free time for swim or rest before lunch and then it was right back to concert practice in the afternoon. This was followed by sectional practice before mail call and another half-hour swim or rest time and then dinner. I think we had concert practice in the evening too, some time planned for group social activity, and then vespers around the campfire before bedtime. Taps sounded around 9 p.m. It was a full and regimented schedule, the same every day, and by the end of the week, some of us were ready to break out.

One summer a certain small mixed-gender group did plan an illicit "after-taps rendezvous" in the woods. But Myers got wind of it and just as lights-out was happening, he got on his bullhorn outside and declared to the row of cabins, in no uncertain terms, he would cancel our trip to march in the parade at Chicago's Riverview Park the following week if anyone sneaked out that night. We knew he wasn't bluffing and for sure no one dared defy his edict.

Myers ran a tight ship. Bandsmen did not act out. It was not appropriate. We were expected to be models of decorum. I don't think it was explicitly stated. We understood this by his example. We knew he would be gravely displeased if we behaved otherwise and we didn't want to be responsible for that happening. He was in his mid-thirties in the sixties, full of energy, motivated to make his mark and my compatriots and I were the beneficiaries. Band camp was just the beginning. He took us off to marching competitions, band days at Western, Michigan State and U of M. There were parades at home and other places, with the big prize at Riverview Park when we were cut loose to enjoy the amusements after our marching detail was finished. Then two big Greyhound buses waited to carry us back home.

There must have been oodles of blurry eyes the next morning for parents who picked us up in the wee hours when those buses finally pulled into the high school parking lot. But band parents were a dedicated lot. In fact, one parent in particular went well beyond during the summer of '62, when we needed warm-weather uniforms. Our wool red coats were too heavy for summer wear, so we pieced together more comfortable though not especially snappy gear. We wore white short-sleeve collared shirts, black bermuda-length shorts, white knee socks and black shoes. Yeah, the look was boring. It needed a boost. So Norrine Myers, spouse to our illustrious director, came up with a nifty design. Then Susan Reits' mother, who was handy with a needle, produced seventy, yes SEVENTY, bright red pleated cummerbunds with side sashes to match. The sashes hung to the knee and were finished off by white tassels on the ends. Thanks to Mrs. Myers' creativity and Mrs. Reits' devotion, the splash of handsome red needlework transformed our black and white ensemble into one impressive outfit.

Band camp, concert practice, marching practice, college band days, parades, half-time shows, competitions and concerts in the park... how many times did we lug our gear across the footbridge at Maple Isle? How many times did we set up on Courthouse Square? How many times did we stand in heavy wool red coats in the sun listening to Memorial Day speeches? And no one complained. What makes kids persist like this? Why do they sign on for such a commitment? Experts say that band membership breeds an ability to stick with a chosen path, whatever it might be. They also say that self-confidence, esprit de corps, and willingness to work hard toward a goal come from spending time with the band. But are these the reasons why kids choose band for themselves? I asked a few of my former bandmates what drove them to join so long ago. They said that the benefits listed by the experts were accurate outcomes for their own experience in band, but not the motivators that drove their decisions to join. Rather, to a person, instead they said: "I love music".

As I look back on my own reasons for choosing band, one of them was that I like music too and I wanted to master all those flashy silver keys. Yet, for me, the absolute definitive attraction was the drama: the red coats and shiny horns, the cadence, big kids marching in step in neatly dressed rows, the drum major's whistle and fancy baton. The attire, the precision, the big sound, being part of the show! That's what I wanted. To me, all these things put together shouted out: "Here we come, the proud children of our great little town!" And that's how it felt...the Paw Paw spirit. It still lives, you know...enduring over generations and supported by memories and words like these...a joyous record of yesterday...when we wore the Red Coats.

# 'The Summer of 1964: Innocence Interrupted'

The summer of '64 started out in much the same way as the one before. I was running with a "pack" of about eight or nine other girls. We were friends since junior high school, "thick as thieves" and headed into our junior year with that notorious adolescent "know-it-all" attitude. Our WWII veteran parents told us: "Just work hard and you can have it all. Anything is possible." They saved the free world from tyranny and hatred only twenty years before and they really believed that hard work and self-application would always pay off. So we believed *them* and assumed the world was our oyster.

Our world at that time was a little town called Paw Paw located about half-way between Detroit and Chicago. The old saying goes: "Paw Paw: the town so nice they named it twice," And just as "they" also say, it was "a great place to raise a family." Sandy soil, built up over the centuries from Lake Michigan, was perfect for growing cherries, peaches, pears, apples and grapes. Farm machinery was in demand, canning factories hummed along, wineries flourished and the Welch's Grape Juice processing factory was just down the road.

Paw Paw is the Van Buren County seat and boasts a stately Greek Classical-style copper-domed courthouse flanked on both sides by Civil War cannon. A block-long promenade leads to the main entrance. When I was a kid, attorneys and county officials bustled about on the streets around it everyday. They mixed with merchants and other business owners meeting up at "The Grill," "Hamburg Haven" or the "Hotel De Hamburger," for lunch or coffee.

The courthouse as I remember it. Postcard image circa 1950.

One lonely stoplight hung over the center of town at the intersection of Michigan Rt. 40 and U.S. 12. The Main Street business district extended from that junction about three blocks east to west and the same length north to south. Interstate I-94 passed by about a half-mile south of town in 1961, and that cut down on through traffic. But there was still plenty of hustle in town, with people tending to the needs of our farm families.

Farm life was primary in Paw Paw and a source of pride especially apparent at the Post Office. The building is simple and stately, designed by Louis Simon and erected in 1939 as part of an economic stimulus project. It sits one block north of the traffic light and is especially important because it shelters an impressive piece of artwork inside just above the postmaster's office door. It's a huge mural painted in 1940 by Carlos Lopez, one of many American artists enlisted by FDR to adorn federal buildings with depictions of American life. There was competition for the work and Lopez won with a design he called *Bounty*. *Bounty* captures the rural dignity and humanity of Southwestern Michigan farm life with bold images and brilliant colors. The painting was completed well before my birth and, as far as I was concerned, it always existed in that space like a "constant," something I could count on. When I was small there was no problem in waiting for Mom while she did her business at the service window. I just looked up and got lost in the colors and joyful figures of *Bounty*. I scanned it inch by inch, always discovering something not seen before.

*Bounty*, Carlos Lopez, 1940   Image courtesy of photographer Dirk Bakker, copyright 1979.

FDR intended the works as decoration for sure. But he wanted them to be sources of inspiration for future generations too and that is exactly what *Bounty* was for me. My aesthetic side was "moved" by that painting. "Bounty" was most likely my introduction to the art world, and I still love to look at it.

Greyhound buses made regular stops across the street and down the alley behind Wilson's News Service. This was a busy place with all manner of folks coming and going. Bus passengers departed and arrived at least a couple of times a day and busy paper boys folded and packed up daily issues of the *Kalamazoo Gazette* in the back room, then took off on bicycles in every direction tossing deliveries onto front porches all over town. Julius Forbes was the proprietor, and he kept his racks stocked with up-to-date print media. If I had a dime, I checked in most every week at age 9 or 10 to see if the latest issue of *Superman* was there. I couldn't get enough of this superhero with a double life who did so much good for people. It was a fascination and I have to wonder if this comic book hero inspired my career choices later in life. Using whatever power I can muster to make a difference for other folks seems almost second nature to me.

Forbes, a man of stern countenance and a Groucho Marx look-alike, held court behind the smoke supplies counter where he kept cigars, cigarettes, pipes, pouches of loose tobacco, papers for folks who liked to roll their own and, I suppose, plugs for chewing. Dad smoked a pipe once in a while when he tried to cut back on Chesterfield cigarettes and Mom did her best to help out with this plan by picking up a pouch of cherry blend to ease his cravings. I must have tagged along on her mission, and that was likely my introduction to this most interesting of places. To say the least, I loved it. On the wall rack opposite his tobacco products, Forbes kept rows of daily papers, magazines, paperback novels, trade journals and comic books. This is where I lingered, scanning everything, hoping to find fresh new adventures about the "Man of Steel." The air was heavy with the scent of newsprint, and I suppose this is the reason why I still prefer hard copy with my morning coffee. The smell and feel of it most likely serve as comforts against disturbing news of the day.

Breedveld's Shoe Shop was a little further on down the alleyway and I always entered from the back. I passed by dozens of shoe boxes and the workroom where owner Jud Dannenberg must have colored at least a half dozen pairs of linen shoes for me to match two prom dresses and three or four bridesmaid's gowns. Jud worshiped with us at the First Presbyterian Church and helped out with youth fellowship field trips and church suppers. He knew me by name and always seemed pleased to see me.

Ollie Dreier, one of Dad's contemporaries, managed Harding's Supermarket on the next block and down the street from Jud's shop. "Ollie's boy, Billy," as my dad called him, worked at the store on weekends and lived next door to my friend Debbie Clair. He noticed me at Debbie's house one day in 1960 and I was surprised and thrilled. He was small, with an athletic build, and mature enough to shave his facial hair. The smell of aftershave lingered when he held my hand and made me feel very "grown up." Billy was kind and funny, and we spent the better part of my seventh grade school year as a couple in a typical adolescent puppy love thing. I was 13 and he was 14. We went to the movies on Saturday afternoons at the Strand Theater in town, and after the show we stepped across the street to the "Hotel De Hamburger," a little joint converted from an old streetcar, owned and operated by Chuck Sage, one of Dad's pals. Chuck and his wife Joyce tended the counter, and I could count on a warm greeting when I showed up there, too. They had a jukebox and celebrity photos of Sinatra, Lewis and Martin, Monroe, Gleason, Benny Goodman and others on the walls. The place had a grill and a few booths for dining. Burgers, chips, ice cream, shakes, and soda pop were all they served. The burger recipe was a well guarded family secret and the best in town!

When Billy and I went out at night, ice skating, roller skating, or to basketball games, Ollie was our chauffeur. For swimming at the lake we rode our bikes. I loved Billy, and all was right with the world as long as he was around. The feeling must have been mutual. He made a ring for me in shop class from a cross-section of copper pipe and presented it with much pride. It was too big for my finger, so I wrapped angora yarn around it like the older girls did with their beaux' class rings. I loved wearing it and showing it off even though it eventually made my finger turn green. I reciprocated his symbol of devotion with a cheap medallion I picked up at the county fair. It had my name engraved on it and he wore it on a chain around his neck. Billy and I were going steady and everyone knew it. There wasn't anything more to it than holding hands and smooching in the back row at the Strand. It was all "very proper" compared to what goes on with teenagers today, but it was big stuff to me. This was the seventh grade in 1961! Definitely a different era.

Despite my liaison with "Ollie Dreier's boy," Mom didn't do her grocery shopping at Harding's Market. She preferred another store called the "Shopping Center" right across the street. It was like a general store with groceries plus apparel, toys and games. My first bra came from the Shopping Center and the butcher there, Lyle Cross, knew Mom by name. "Barb, what do you need today?" he said as Mom inspected the chops, steaks and roasts in Lyle's display case. Prepackaged meats had not yet been born, so Mom made her selections and Lyle weighed, wrapped and delivered exactly what she wanted.

Her allegiance to this store may have started from the day she won the grand opening door prize. As I understand the story, clerks appeared out of nowhere, escorted her down every aisle and filled her cart to overflowing with all manner of complimentary goods. This happened in the '50s which was a rather lean time for my folks. Dad was struggling to make a go of his business, the Paw Paw Sawmill, James E. Jennings, Proprietor. Mom kept the books and met payroll while at home with my sister Kay and me. I mention this because the outcome of the shopping spree yielded some items that were much more exotic than what usually appeared on our pantry shelves. There were things like canned lobster and other delicacies uncommon in the Midwest and so a curiosity to me.

My best friend was a farm kid named Judy Woodman. The Woodmans were land rich, with several branches of the family tree spread out all over the county still farming orchards and vineyards passed down over generations. With Judy in my life, new horizons opened up. There were tractors and wagons to ride on and acres of grass and trees to roam, not to mention barns to explore. One of those barns was used to store a special plaything, a 1937 green Ford pick-up truck carefully preserved from the elder Woodman's courtship days. It still ran great, was useful for chores around the farm, and was appropriated frequently by us for joy rides on orchard roads late at night. With Judy, there was plenty of mischief, and those days are rich with happy memories.

Everyone I knew drove Fords or GM cars. This was Michigan after all. My folks bought Chevys as a rule, guaranteed to rust out from harsh Michigan winters and destined to be replaced every three years because of it. We bought them from Dad's pal, John Tapper, a hotshot salesman with Harrison Chevrolet. Eventually Tapper joined Henderson's Oldsmobile Pontiac dealership on the west side of town and in 1963 Mom and Dad abandoned Harrison and bought an Oldsmobile F-85 Coupe. Maybe this was a signal they were moving up. I guess I was moving up too, since I had a driver's license by the time the Olds was parked in our garage and I used it to get around town.

That's the car I was driving when I got clocked doing 40 mph in a 30 mph zone along the lake one night on my way home. I didn't get stopped. Our local cop just let Dad know it happened and I heard about it over dinner a few days later. I got the message to slow down and of course never again exceeded the speed limit---at least not on that stretch of road.

That's the way it was. People looked out for each other and for each other's kids. It's one of the advantages of small town life. Or maybe not. There was little privacy and virtually no anonymity.

There are two lakes within the Paw Paw Village limits. Maple Lake is the largest, fed by a branch of the Paw Paw River that runs right between the business district and where I went to high school. The State Police Post still sits on the lake's southern shore now, overlooking a concert bowl where folks gather on summer nights for live music and to watch the swans. Yes, we had swans, and they occasionally strayed onto the streets. Dad worked for the DPW and from time to time he was called upon to herd the swans back from whence they came. Apparently swans can be nasty and the herding task unpleasant, as I came to understand from the play-by-play accounts shared later over dinner on those days.

I spent the better part of my summers swimming, water skiing and otherwise playing by that lake with Billy, Judy and other pals, just as Dad did when he was a youngster. Paw Paw was Dad's hometown. His maternal ancestors were among the earliest of settlers in Van Buren County during the 1830s and '40s. He was a star athlete in school and a skilled swimmer. He taught me to swim at his folks' place on Ackley Lake, just north of town where Gommie, Pa, Aunt Irene, Uncle Carl (Hover, from Bangor), a slew of cousins, and extended family gathered at the old homestead on the lake most weekends.  We picnicked with Pa's homemade lemonade, lots of yummy things brought from home for everyone to share, and fresh frog legs caught from the lake by Pa, Dad and Uncle Carl.  Cousin Jimmy built his own speedboat and the older cousins took turns water-skiing.  Cousin Dickie and I were about the same age, great playmates and the youngest of all Gommie's grandchildren.  Sometimes Dickie and I got to visit with Gommie by ourselves, and she let us use her rowboat and showed us how to fish with bamboo poles on lazy summer afternoons.   We used salvaged black inner tubes for swimming and horsing around in the water.   Then we changed out of our swimsuits in the barn. Gommie rigged up a "changing area" there under her vintage "Chew Mail Pouch Tobacco" signs that hung on the walls.  This plan cut down on beach sand in the house and saved her a lot of housekeeping headaches.

There are tales to be told about life around those lakes. After the war, Dad and his G.I. pals fashioned a leisure watercraft from a war surplus rubber raft, attached a wooden floor, a canopy and an outboard motor, added a few chairs and tables, and launched the first pontoon boat ever seen on Maple Lake. They docked this craft at Chuck and Joyce Sage's lake-front landing and the *Kalamazoo Gazette* came out to do a feature story complete with photos. The paper called the project "A Floating Front Porch" and compared it to the storied Stork Club lounge in New York City.

During the summer of '64, I carried on Dad's legacy of fun on the water.  Our home was north of town and across M-40 from the eastern shoreline of Maple Lake.  Mary Jane Dillon lived in the neighborhood, and her family had a speedboat docked down the road.  M.J., the rest of the gang and I joined in on a regular basis skiing behind that boat and playing on the mile-long lake all summer long.

Once in a while, we met up with Sheldon Rupert, Jr., another one of our classmates, who liked to play on the water too. Shelly's dad was one of the attorneys who hustled in and out of the courthouse downtown, and the Rupert family had a lovely home on the northwest shoreline of the big lake. Despite his small and slight stature, Shelly was an emerging athlete. He mastered the high dive installed atop the Rupert family raft and was loved for his signature "Rooster Tail" slalom. His ski had a hole at the back to allow a column of spray to shoot out from his heels as he raced behind the speeding boat with his best pal, Donny Hall, at the wheel. It was a neat show, visible at least 100 yards or more across the lake and people noticed.

Everyone in town knew Shelly. He made his reputation as a local hero in 1962, at age 14, when he and Donny discovered a capsized craft one night that summer after watching fireworks from the water. Shelly dived in and located two bodies right away. Two more were recovered the next morning. Two beloved priests from Saint Mary's parish, Father Anthony Wade and Father Clarence Wood, along with Veronica Lange, a local parishioner, and Father Raymond Fleissner, a visiting priest from Illinois, all drowned that night. Apparently this group went out onto the lake to view the fireworks too and something went terribly wrong. These losses left our little community in shock, grief and confusion for decades. Details were never clear and the event remains  the worst water tragedy in Paw Paw history.

Given Shelly's heroics and athletic prowess, some of the girls in our gang started noticing him with a good bit of interest that was tragically cut short when we lost him, too. There was a terrible accident on the Crocker farm in July.  The emergency medical team did what they could, but Shelly's injuries were severe and he died within hours at Lakeview Hospital. John Fleming, another classmate and longtime friend, witnessed the gruesome aftermath. Even now, more than fifty years later, John recalls vivid images from what he saw that day.

Isn't it amazing how some sights, sounds or smells endure like that? Those of a certain age can remember with clarity exactly where they were or what they were doing when word came of the JFK assassination, or more recently, when the twin towers fell on 9/11. It's commonly called "flashbulb memory," a term coined more than a decade after John's mind recorded the grisly scene. The phenomenon has been captured using brain scans. So it is established: connections between emotion and biology are quite real, and trauma transforms our enduring physical makeup.

I wasn't at Shelly's accident scene, but it seems I too have a bit of flashbulb memory associated with events during the few days that followed. I can recall with clarity, from July of 1964, the painful expression on Oradell Rupert's face as she watched her son's classmates file into Hawley's Funeral Home for the obsequies and again when we flooded the scene at Wildey Cemetery for Shelly's burial. It was an emotion-packed time for our tight-knit community.

At such a tender age and in this otherwise idyllic setting, it took a while for us to wrap our minds around how fragile and unfair life can be. Whenever we were gathered at the lake following his death, the expectation remained that Shelly's rooster tail would somehow magically appear "any time now" whizzing across the waves just like always. The 1962 drownings were bad enough, but the loss of our schoolmate two years later was exceptionally hard to accept and I suppose especially so for Donny and Shelly's good pal, Bob Crocker Jr. We were sad and frightened. It seemed our community and way of life within it were not as safe and secure as we believed.

This was the beginning of a pivotal time. Within the next few years, Bob Jr. and Donny would go off to fight an insidious, impossible war on the other side of the world. More civil unrest would erupt in the Deep South. Two horrible political assassinations and huge changes in social mores on campuses across the nation would shake things up in a thousand ways. Our gang would be pushed to expand our ways of thinking and of handling challenge.

But in the summer of 1964, after Shelly died, we were in no way ready for the tests, complexities and vulnerabilities of adulthood. Rather, stability and predictability were probably the most important things on our minds. So we turned to our families and each other for support and protection to beat a retreat back to more carefree and familiar diversions. We had band camp, church camp, sleepovers in the back yard and dancing on the beach to tunes by a new British group called the Beatles. These were the things we knew best, the things that made us happy. It was our way to cope, to salvage, for just a little while longer, a trace of our innocence so rudely interrupted. Then we soldiered on...still the same kids, though certainly forever changed by the summer of 1964.

The courthouse clock tower stood empty for eighty years until Oradell and Sheldon Rupert Sr. provided for the purchase of the lighted dial shown below.

Image of Van Buren County Courthouse reproduced courtesy of Brent McNitt, 1001 Words Photography, Paw Paw, Michigan, copyright 2018.

# 'Maple Isle'

In the spring of 1955 I was among the first wave of Paw Paw baby boomers to finish up our first-grade school year during the first year that Paw Paw Elementary School on Cedar Street was open for business. Now, those are a lot of firsts. But to top it all off, we were excited about our first end-of-year class picnic. We dressed in our play clothes that day—shorts and sneakers (otherwise known as tennis shoes in the Midwest). As I recall, each of us brought a packed lunch from home, piled onto a school bus and traveled a mile north of town for fun and games with our teacher, Louise Myers, away from the usual classroom humdrum.

Michigan Route 40 northbound was a two-laner in those days, and I suppose the mile-long ride seemed to take forever in the minds of that busload of six-year-old kids. All these things made the outing a special occasion—a significant rite of passage—in a significant setting. Our destination was Maple Isle, a familiar spot to most of us.

We were a bunch of townies. The farm kids still went to one-room country schoolhouses in those days. All of us at the Paw Paw Elementary School on Cedar Street lived within walking distance of most every attraction within the village limits. Maple Isle lay just at the edge of those limits---a summer playground that was a "constant" for us. "The Island," as it was known to the locals, was in existence for as long as we could remember, so of course we assumed it had been there forever. But indeed, that was not the case.

Maple Isle was born in 1907 when village officials gave the order and the Paw Paw River was dammed to provide much-

71

needed electrical current for our town. The beautiful mile-long lake named Maple was a by-product of that flood and a natural high spot in the terrain remaining above the lake surface would later be christened "Maple Isle."

For decades this five-acre survivor of the deluge remained high and dry, inhabited by wild migratory birds and only accessible by boat. But in 1939, a wooden footbridge was installed connecting this piece of ground to the mainland. That bridge was built barely ten years before I was born and just about 15 years before my first-grade picnic outing. In the greater scheme of things, 15 years is not a long time, but that particular 15-year span does represent a very significant time for the village, and the start of a 40-year-long heyday for the park.

Maple Isle was perfect for mid-20th-century Paw Paw. During the Great Depression and the war years, spending for leisure was impossible. So the Island was great entertainment. Picnics and swimming at the lake were accessible, fun and free. Town families lived within walking distance. Virtually no one had a swimming pool in those days and few had air conditioning even into the '70s. If you wanted to cool off, you went to the lake. If you didn't have lake front property, you went to "The Island."

On weekends, both early on and then after I came along, the place was a popular family picnic spot and a destination for out-of-towners, too. One of my friends who pumped gas on weekends during high school days tells me that folks routinely stopped at the station to ask: "Which way to Maple Isle?". Actually, there were so many cars headed for the place in the '50s and '60s that when all those travelers finally reached the Island entrance, parking was a big challenge. Families searched for space up and down the shoulders of M-40 to the north and south of the bridge. There were parked cars lined up on east and west sides of the road for as far as you could see. Then, once a space was found, travelers could be seen toting folding beach chairs, picnic baskets, swim gear, plus kids from car to bridge early in the day and back again as evening approached.

When I was little, maybe four or five or even six, seven, or eight, there was a bait shop along the highway at the base of the footbridge and boats of all descriptions pulled in and out by the gas pump to fill up for a day of fishing or water skiing. The bait shop had a boat launch too. Folks fortunate enough to own boats could put in right there, cruise across the channel to the south side of the island, claim their picnic spot on land, and settle in for a day of boating and family fun. There was even a baseball diamond for anyone who wanted to get up a game and a large sheltered pavilion so sudden changes in weather didn't have to spoil anyone's fun. The only downside was in one particular spot, the migrating geese continued a presence. Goose droppings were always abundant there, so the human park patrons knew to steer clear.

The most common way to access the island was by way of the footbridge and on warm summer days the wooden planks on that bridge got hot enough to scald my tender little feet if I tried to cross without shoes or sandals. This circumstance made me ornery because, to me, the island was synonymous with going barefoot and I was stubborn about retaining that kind of freedom. But some of my young comrades also suffered splinter wounds from those same planks, so I reluctantly yielded and put on my shoes before traipsing the treacherous track back to the mainland.

When I was about ten or eleven, Bill Bollinger offered swimming lessons at the Island on summer mornings, and I signed up. Bill was one of several lifeguards who kept watch over throngs of kids in the afternoons from one of two lifeguard platforms—one for the little kids' swim area and the other for older youngsters. The lifeguards had a lifesaving boat, and there were two rafts that floated on oil barrel pontoons anchored some yards off shore. These were within a designated, roped and buoyed swim area maybe twenty-five yards square off the north shore. We could swim out to a raft, climb up the ladder, rest a while, check out who was there and if we didn't like the company, jump or dive off and visit the other raft.

On weekdays the place was crawling with youngsters of all ages. Young moms had their little ones in tow with sand pails and shovels. Bigger kids rode their bikes from town with towels thrown over their shoulders. High school kids hung out at the concession stand behind the bathhouse—not so much interested in swimming, and way more interested in who looked best in a bathing suit or whose tan was deeper than anyone else's. Of course, there was plenty of courting going on, too. In our teens, Billy Dreier and I spread out beach towels together in some secluded spot and the Island's west shoreline was a great location for anyone who wanted to check out who was skiing or sailing on the lake.

One of my last memories of Maple Isle involved a boat outing. I was about 20, so it must have been around 1968. Judy Woodman and I were sailing a little Sun-fish type craft off the Island's north shoreline when we came across our classmate Debbie Clair and friends in another boat. We shared some fun time with them and they shared their bottle of Boone's Farm Apple wine with us. There was just as much happening on the Island that day as I have described above and I figure if I was witnessing that kind of thing 20 years after the beginning of the baby boom, then those who came along at the end of the boom were most likely making similar use of Maple Isle until at least around 1980. After that, the Island seems to have started a slow decline in activity.

Maple Isle footbridge just as I remember it.  Postcard image circa 1950.

Maple Isle famously met Paw Paw's recreational needs immediately before the war and for a good long while thereafter. But it seems today's story is vastly different. I went back to Paw Paw in 2016 for my 50th high school class reunion and walked the footbridge once again. The old bridge is no more. No splintered, heat-retaining planks.  The whole expanse is now completely replaced, made from more durable stuff. The bait shop and gas pump are long gone and M-40 is now a four-lane highway. Parking on the shoulders is not possible these days due to highway curbing and actually seems a non-issue. The park is still: no lifeguards, no swimming, no rafts on oil drum pontoons. The bathhouse is there, but with no concession stand around back, no throngs of children running and jumping in the water. The setting is quiet. Boomers are aging. Young families are fewer. Air conditioning is common, and many have swimming pools at home. The Island is preserved and promoted still as a town park for recreation, while slowly being reclaimed by the migratory birds who once dominated the same space a full century ago.

So am I sad and tearful that a significant and joyful period in history is no longer? Absolutely not! Instead, I'm smiling inside and out. I'm smiling in celebration of that time, celebrating that it happened, that I got to participate and that I can share this record of what it was like "way back when." Maple Isle was a source of joy for our collective families, joy that will live on in stories like these passed down through generations.

Dear reader, please know that you too can share in this joy no matter what your age or era. Please, please, the next time you pass by Prospect Hill, St. Mary's, or any other Paw Paw community cemetery, ask yourself: "How many of those souls laid there to rest shared laughter with friends, swam to the rafts, enjoyed summer picnics, launched boats, played with their kids, or even fell in love at Maple Isle?"

Dear reader, are you smiling?

# *Afterword*

These vignettes, I believe, reflect the flavor of a particular time in the history of my little town with the funny name. Paw Paw is one of those places where proud, brave people lived, labored, laughed, loved and left their legacies for the rest of us. This is my humble attempt to immortalize the names and character of a few quite ordinary, everyday people who made an extraordinary difference for the many in my hometown…a record from one who went before, to those who will come after…a window on a different time in a special place.

There are more stories out there about pioneers much like Ben and Sally Eager. There are more tales of courage about war heroes and cool memories from school days and growing up in Paw Paw or other places quite like it. My intent is that these vignettes reveal the power of small-town life, reinforce pride in collective heritage, and perhaps inspire readers to take the time to dig way down, resurrect, and then record their own stories before it is too late. Please do it. Share the stories, reflections of Arthur Morgan's "elemental traits—neighborliness, fair play, courage, tolerance, open minded inquiry, patience." Tell those who will come after about how, once upon a time, these were passed on from one generation to the next in our small communities— Morgan's "seedbeds of [American] society."

M.L. Jennings, 2020

# Acknowledgements

A piece of work like this one cannot be done adequately in complete solitude. I am deeply indebted to dear friends for extremely valuable support during this process. For fact-checking and much needed detail needed to fill in my memory gaps, a big thank you goes to longtime friends and neighbors from Paw Paw days: John Fleming, Judy Woodman, Sherry Sage Helmich, Linda Myers Schwalm, Larry Ward, Wendy Ball McCormick, Tom Oldfield, Linda Woodman Tulusius, Joyce Sage, Mary Adams and Robert (Butch) Hindenach.

Much appreciated support came from The Memoirs Writing Group weekly meetings at the Holyoke, Massachusetts Senior Center. Dian McCullum, Connie Lavelle, Jo McNulty, Eula Walter, Nancy Laferriere, Charlie Cavagnac and Peter Mollo all kindly tolerated endless readings and rewrites and offered ever-encouraging personal feedback and suggestions that made a huge impact on the way ideas were expressed in each of these stories. Their help was immeasurable.

Appreciation goes to the following for granting permission to reprint copyrighted materials:

Dirk Bakker, *Bounty*, copyright 1979.

Brent McNitt, *Van Buren County Courthouse at Night*, copyright 2018.

*Mlive Media Group/Kalamazoo Gazette*, *Raft of Fun* by Dan Ryan, circa 1949.

Paw Paw Public Schools, architectural rendering of Cedar Street Elementary School, *Wappaw, 1953.*

Special thanks go to the following: my colleague Barbara Dautrich, retired Professor of Education, American Internatinal College for much-needed expert counsel on the era of "Learning by Doing" in *And the Old Shall be New Again* which proved to be an exceptionally challenging chapter;  to Joyce Belliveau for graciouly agreeing to produce an amusing depiction of the U.S.S. Salvage; to Patricia Fake for capturing the exact image I envisioned for the cover; and to Joanne Despres for much essential editorial expertise.

Finally, to those who persevered through countless (and I mean countless) rewrites and proofreadings.  I am forever indebted to Connie Ashcraft, my dear friend from Paw Paw High School; my neighbor Marc Prince who, praise the Lord, thrives in his role as constructive critic; my sister, Kay Jennings Fox, for actually being there as first hand witness to much of what I write; and my partner in life, Victoriah Hall, for her unwavering encouragement and belief in my ability to really make this happen.


Thank you, all.

# References

Carson, C.C., Huelskamp, R.M. & Woodell, T.D.,(1993). Perspectives on education in America. *Journal of Educational Research*, Sandia National Laboratories, 86 (5).

Dewey, J., (1916). *Democracy and education*: An introduction to the philosophy of education. New York, MacMillan.

Falan, W., (1999). Personal communication and Paw Paw High School athletic records for 1931-1934.

Ganzel, B. (2007). Farming in the '50s and '60s: television. http://livinghistoryfarm.org/farminginthe80s/life_17. html.

Hindenach, R.R., (2020). *Tales, legends, myths and notable citizens of Paw Paw, Michigan*. Pawpawwappaw.com.

Morgan, A., (1942). The community: The seedbed of society. *Atlantic*.

Murrow, E.R., (1958). 'Wires and lights in a Box'. Speech delivered at Radio and TV News Directors' Association Convention, Chicago.

Paw Paw, Michigan U.S. Decennial Census Population Data 1950 and 1960 (2020).

*Portraits and biographical records of Kalamazoo, Allegan and VanBuren Counties, Michigan*. (1892). Chicago: Chapman Brothers.

Rogers, J.B., (1959). *Footpaths to freeways Paw Paw centennial pictorial history souvenir program*, Paw Paw, Michigan: Centennial Association.

U.S. Census Bureau (2019). 1950s: TV and Radio. Retrieved from http://www.encyclopedia.com.

U.S. Department of Education, (1983). National Commission on Excellence in Education, *'A nation at risk'*. Washington, D.C.: GPO.

# Name Index

# About the Author

Martha L. Jennings is a 1966 graduate of Paw Paw High School. She received a B.A. from Western Michigan University in 1970 and an M.A. in 1971. Mart spent seven years as a counselor at the Good Samaritan Hospital School of Nursing in Cincinnati, Ohio before earning an Ed.D. in Counseling Psychology from Indiana University in 1981. She served as a psychologist at Wittenberg University from 1981 until 1988 and Professor of Psychology at American International College from 1988 until 2011. Mart is happily retired, lives in Springfield, Massachusetts and loves reading, writing, cooking and spending time with Paw Paw friends.

Made in the USA
Middletown, DE
08 January 2021